AT THE SHARP END

AT THE
SHARP END
From Le Paradis to Kohima

2nd Battalion
The Royal Norfolk Regiment

Peter Hart

Pen & Sword Books Limited, Barnsley
LEO COOPER

DEDICATED TO THE
MEMORY OF
'WINKIE' FITT
1919-1997
REGIMENTAL SERGEANT
MAJOR
ROYAL NORFOLK REGIMENT

First published in Great Britain in 1998 by Leo Cooper
an imprint of Pen & Sword Books Limited
47 Church Street, Barnsley, South Yorkshire S70 2AS

Copyright © Peter Hart, 1998

*For up-to date information on other titles
produced under the Pen & Sword imprint,
please telephone or write to:*
Pen & Sword Books Limited
FREEPOST
47 Church Street
Barnsley
South Yorkshire
S70 2BR

Telephone (24 hours): 01226 734555

ISBN 0-85052-635-3

British Library Cataloguing in Publication Data

**Printed by Redwood Books Ltd
Trowbridge, Wiltshire**

2940

Contents

Fitt and his platoon in the Kohima area.

Preface

I am greatly indebted to the old comrades of the 2nd Battalion, Royal Norfolk Regiment without whom this book would not exist. The Royal Norfolk Regiment Sound Recording project to which they contributed was initiated by The Imperial War Museum Sound Archive in conjunction with Major Reeve of the Royal Norfolk Regimental Association and Kate Thaxton of Royal Norfolk Regimental Museum. Yet it was the veterans themselves which made the project so exciting and by patiently tape recording their memories provided the raw material. All I have done is to choose the best extracts from their interviews and then tried to link them together within a broad historical context. I therefore must particularly thank – in alphabetical order – **Stan Banks, Peter Barclay, Dennis Boast, R Brown, Len Brazier, Arthur Brough, Len Chamberlain, William Cron, Dickie Davies, Ernie Farrow, Dick Fiddament, Bert Fitt, Maurice Franses, Walter Gilding, Fred Hazell, Sam Hornor, John Howard, Ernie Leggett, Herbert Lines, Ben Macrae, John Mather, Bert May, Bill Robinson, Stan Roffey, Fred Rolleston, Jack Russell** and **Bill Seymour**. It is true that not all are widely quoted in this particular book, but they all played a vital part in building this archive which I am sure others will use to far greater effect in the future.

I would also like to thank my charming and exceptionally able colleagues in the Imperial War Museum Sound Archive. Margaret Brooks, Kate Johnson, Laura Kamel, Rosemary Tudge and Conrad Wood have, by dint of sheer hard work, amassed an archive which is without doubt the finest summation of human experience and knowledge in the face of the misery and challenge of war. Of course I am also particularly grateful to the other interviewers who assisted in the actual recording programme i.e. Nigel de Lee and Stuart Pentecost. Elsewhere in the IWM my trusty chums Nigel Steel from the Department of Documents and Bryn Hammond of Information Systems have been indefatigable in proof checking and improving this text. Ron Brooker, Ian Carter and Paul Coleman of the IWM Photographic Archive were extremely helpful in providing copies and giving me permission to reproduce many of the photographs in the text. Many of the other photographs were supplied by the veterans themselves, particularly Maurice Franses and John Howard.

As a fellow museum worker I can only express my bemused wonderment at the dedicated efficiency of Kate Thaxton and her team at the Royal Norfolk Regimental Museum in Norwich. Under funded, as they undoubtedly are, they nevertheless achieve miracles and I would recommend anyone interested in this great regiment to pay them a visit. They provided both documentary and photographic support for this book. Major William Reeve of the Anglian Regiment and Major Sam Hornor were also kind enough to read advance copies of the manuscript which prevented many 'howlers' for which I am deeply grateful.

Finally, but by no means least, Roni Wilkinson of Pen & Sword was chief designer, editor, friend, cook and bottlewasher and should definitely have his salary massively increased if there is not to be a serious injustice! [*He also typeset this page – Ed.*] It could be said with some justice that perhaps all I am solely responsible for in this book are any remaining blunders!

The extracts have been lightly edited and re-ordered only where necessary to improve readability or clarity. The general accuracy of the information within the quotations has been checked against the regimental history and the relevant war diaries in the Public Record Office. The original tapes are available for consultation by appointment at The IWM Sound Archive, Lambeth Road, London SE1 6HZ. Telephone for an appointment: 0181-416-5363.

Peter Hart
Oral Historian, IWM
January, 1998

Left: *A contemporary print dipicting men of the 9th East Norfolk Regiment during the Napoleonic Wars.*
Above: *The 9th in action during the Sikh Wars – the Battle of Moodkee 1846.*
Below: *Muleteers of the 8th Battalion in 1915.*

The 9th Foot, subsequently the Royal Norfolk Regiment, was raised by James II in 1685. It went on to fight all over the world and figured extensively in the actions of the Peninsular War. After the French had been driven out of Spain the 9th was sent to Canada and so missed the final battle against Napoleon at Waterloo. A stint in the West Indies was the cause of heavy casualties through disease and they returned from those fever climes in 1827 a mere fragment of their normal strength. India followed and the Afghan Wars, then the fighting against the Sikhs. March 1854 and England declared war on Russia and the 9th were launched into the Crimean war where disease laid low far more than enemy action. In 1857 the 9th became a two-battalion regiment. As the century came to its close numerous small wars of Empire occupied the Norfolks. The Boer War in particular, where the 2nd Battlion were engaged in the relief of Kimberley, saw many casualties from enteric fever, more so than from Boer rifle fire. During the opening moves of the Great War the 1st Battalion met the Germans head on at Mons. Within weeks the Territorial battalions mobilized and new Kitchener battalions were added to the Regiment. By the end of the First World War the Regiment had lost 5,576 officers and men killed and over 25,000 wounded. Throughout its history the Royal Norfolk Regiment has been renowned for its steadfastness and reliability in difficult situations. A reputation that would be lived up to by another generation of infantrymen who would find themselves at the sharp end in yet another world conflict.

CHAPTER ONE

A Slow Start

For generations the infantry have taken their place at the sharp end of war. In modern combat it is no different. It remains the infantry who must first take and then hold any area of ground whilst engaging the enemy face to face. If they fail then the achievements of other arms will be purely transitory. Artillery and aircraft may smash down defences and destroy communications systems to isolate one particular sector; tanks may crash through and maraud behind the lines. But, unless the infantry occupy the contested area in sufficient strength, then eventually the mobile forces will be forced to withdraw. In the moments that follow the enemy infantry will emerge from their ubiquitous holes in the ground, their reinforcements will flood in, forcing the whole operation to be undertaken all over again. Through these vicious and enervating cycles the bodies mount up.

The skills of the ordinary infantryman given this awful responsibility during the Second World War were of the simple repetitive type. For the most part the average individual could acquire them through basic training alone and after a few weeks could claim to be a soldier, in theory at least, fit to take his place in the line. The harder part, which often took years, was to instil in that soldier the willingness to obey orders in all circumstances, the granite physical toughness to withstand the most appalling discomforts, the underlying courage to face the inevitable consequences of such blind obedience and endurance beyond the point of common sense or self preservation. In essence to do what they were told, when they were told, by whom they were told whatever the prevailing circumstances. Only on achieving this exalted level could the recruit consider himself to have become a British 'regular soldier', a member of an elite corps which stretched back through the smoke of so many grim, sanguinary battles sanitized only in hindsight by the pages of history.

In the inter-war years the sheer physical discomfort and general mayhem experienced by millions of men in the trenches of the Western Front during the First World War cast a dismal shadow over the whole prospect of life in the infantry. A plethora of war poets and miscellaneous literary giants railed in print, sometimes posthumously, against the sacrifice of their generation in that cruellest of wars. Those who

Britannia Barracks in 1936. Soon the buildings and parade ground were teeming with increased activity as the threat of war loomed up again in Europe.

escaped were, by 1939, now grown men with their own children and many had forcefully pointed out to their progeny the awful horrors of war. Yet, undaunted, youth will have its say and many callow young men of 1938 and 1939 had a misplaced confidence in their own immortality. They were ripe to be tempted by the pomp, the circumstance and the sheer youthful zest of army life.

> I was impressed with the service because, my brother, he was stationed at Nelson Barracks which is right near Britannia Barracks. He used to come home with a friend of his – very athletic. Going along the front at Yarmouth doing handsprings, all along the front, he was very fit. And of course that impressed me, I wanted to be like big brother! *Arthur Brough, Great Yarmouth*

Then again civilian life in the late 1930s was not that easy for a working class lad. Although low paid jobs were plentiful in a town like Norwich, the work was often repetitive, boring and lacking in any real prospect of promotion without years of selfless toil for an often ungrateful employer. Some of them realized that they were being bought and sold for coppers.

> I had a second hand cycle and I was biking along the road and I stopped and I have to tell you now, hand on heart, I didn't know where I was working. I'd had so many jobs, I thought, "Where the hell am I going?" I'd forgotten! They weren't really jobs, I wasn't losing anything because you were exploited. Without doubt. In

the butchers' jobs, they used to have half days on Thursday then and the shop would close at one. But you were very, very lucky, especially being a lad if you got out of that shop by 2.30. They were meticulously clean and the blocks had to be scraped and scrubbed etc. The governor would sometimes come along and find fault so you were kept behind for another quarter of an hour. Perhaps you'd got a game of football – so that would spoil it. They were very, very hard times, very demanding. They paid a pittance for wages. I had a reasonable education, I wasn't stupid and learnt very quickly about some things. I certainly knew what was what and I knew I was being exploited, some of them were really unkind and really did take advantage. So there was no reason why I should feel ashamed when I did it for about three days and just never turned up any more. I think there was a lot of my mother in me, she never would be buggered about, I would take so much and that was it. *Dick Fiddament, Norwich*

The regimental depot of the Royal Norfolk Regiment was the old Britannia Barracks built four square in front of the Mousehold common land of the county town of Norwich. To bored town boys and under–paid farm workers its grim walls were ironically a beacon that seemed to offer some kind of escape from the humdrum banalities of their lives. The point of no return came as they were sworn in – the moment at which some of them literally swore their lives away and condemned themselves to war graves far away from home. Most had no idea of the seriousness of the step they were taking and of just how irrevocable it might prove.

> You are given a Bible, you take it and take an oath which roughly goes, "I swear by almighty God my allegiance to His Majesty King George VI, his heirs and successors, etc, etc and you get a shilling – the King's Shilling. One of the lads, Dennis Pitcher, when he enlisted he then turned round to go home, they said, "No, my lad, you're in! You don't go home any more!" *Dick Fiddament, Norwich*

Once they had become soldiers they were assigned to training squads The recruits were held in the barracks until after a couple of weeks there were sufficient to form a training squad of about 30 recruits. Dick Fiddament and Ernie 'Strips' Farrow joined in early 1938 and they were posted together to 105 Squad in the Cameron Block.

> There we met our NCO, Lance Corporal O'Shea. He lectured us about discipline in the army, what we should do, what we shouldn't do. He said that now we were in the army we would be treated as military men and that we'd got to forget that we were ever civilians. If we worked according to how they laid the laws out then we'd have no trouble ever. He really piled it on to us. We

Ernie Farrow

wondered a bit if we'd done the right thing.
Ernie Farrow, 105 Squad, Britannia Barracks,
Before they could think of starting they had to
be kitted out with a uniform and all the basic
equipment for barrack life.

It was the old 1914 uniform, the First
World War. The fit was beautiful. We had
puttees that went all the way up the leg to the
knee, the old ammunition boots, a swagger
cane with a silver knob at the end with the old
Britannia on it, and a pair of gloves. Shirts,
vests, pants, everything like that, you had
three of. The idea they said of that was, "One
pair you wear, one pair goes to the laundry,
and one pair is on inspection". You got PT kit
and you had a khaki overall type of thing for
messing about. *Bert May, Britannia Barracks*
The spartan barrack room which was to be their
new home was in a 'T' shape with beds down the
sides. It had to be spotlessly cleaned every day to
a level which would seem surrealistic in all but

Bert May

the most Victorian of civilian households. The floors were an obvious
starting place for concentrated hard graft.

There would be a huge tin of polish, one of the lads would go
round throwing it on to the floor, then you would work it in with
some rags, then the guy would come along with the bumper – a
thing like a long broom handle quite thick with a heavy thing on
the bottom. You could swing the handle from side to side and you
pulled it towards you then pushed it away and you got into a
rhythm. You could see your reflection in the floor, you could eat
from the floor, it was absolutely spotless. *Dick Fiddament, 105
Squad, Britannia Barracks*
In the centre of the room was a big black cast iron stove and coal bucket.
The combination of coal dust and ashes posed a challenge to the
military mind that was utterly irresistible.

It was similar to boot polish only in a large tin. It was a
composition of lead, jet black. You brushed this on the stove then,
when it dried, you had a larger brush and you polished it. By the
side was a galvanized coal bucket and it was polished to such a
degree that should you be sitting on your bed and the sun
happened to come through the window and catch this you were
virtually blinded! The state of the polishing was magnificent, it
looked like glass, it really did. *Dick Fiddament, 105 Squad,
Britannia Barracks*

It was not only the room that had to be cleaned to perfection. Every article of their equipment and uniform had to be burnished, polished, cleaned and presented 'just so'. In the army 'spit and polish' or 'bull' was not just an expression, it was an altar at which the recruits worshipped daily, with public chastisement for heretics.

The boots were dull black and Lance Corporal O'Shea brought his boots in to show us how they'd got to be. And you could see your face in the toes of his boots. These boots of ours had to be done the same as his before our first parade. He showed us how to do it with the black polish, plenty of spit and the handle of a tooth brush. We put the polish on, a little bit of spit with it and we boned it into the toes of the boots. When the toes were done we had to do the heels. By the time we'd finished we were absolutely knocked up – but we did them and were proud of them. *Ernie Farrow, 105 Squad, Britannia Barracks*

Every day the timetable for the day was posted for each squad on the detail board located at the entrance of the barrack room.

There was a board at the entrance of the barrack room known as the 'detail-board'. It was your duty to read whatever was on there every morning. That would give you a list of the day's happenings. Reveille six o'clock, do your bed, your ablutions, etc, then breakfast, then PT, then possibly it would say, drill from 9.30 for an hour. *Dick Fiddament, 105 Squad, Britannia Barracks*

Frequently they would find that they had to prepare their personal kit for inspection. Everything had to be neatly laid out in a strictly prescribed fashion on their barrack room beds.

You'd look at orders and right at the bottom it might say, "Kit inspection, 0800 hours!" You had to make sure that everything is up to scratch. Your boots are polished lovely, look at the studs at the bottom, they had to be clean, no dirt was allowed on the sole of the shoe and the studs had to be rubbed over with a bit of emery cloth to make sure they were clean, not rusty. Your uniform trousers had to be pressed and laid out, the jacket, then you'd have your shirt folded in a certain way, your socks rolled up, your vest and everything else. At the bottom of the bed you had what you called the holdall. That was a piece of cloth, about eight or nine inches long, about five or six inches wide, with two ties at one end. It had loops and you used to have them laid out properly: knife, fork, spoon, razor, comb, lather brush, button stick, button brush. Then the little envelope at the top was your housewife. That had needles, wool, cotton, buttons. You stood at the bottom of your bed and the Sergeant would come in, or an officer – he would call us all to attention. Then we'd stand at ease and he'd come along each bed and have a look to make sure it was laid out properly. If it wasn't he used to tip it up, "Do it again!" *Bert May, Britannia Barracks*

At breakfast the recruits lined up and prepared to be grateful for the simple, but plentiful, food they were about to receive.

> Most cooks were not very sociable people. As you went past you would have a mug for your tea, a plate, your knife, fork and spoon. You would hold your mug and they would pour in the tea – 'char' – which is the army name. You could stand your spoon up in this, that was really, really strong, you haven't lived until you've tasted army tea. You would then proceed on to the next cook who would look at you inquisitively and you had 'burgoo'(porridge). He would dive the ladle into this quagmire and bang it on your plate – it really was thick stuff. Then you went on and got whatever it was for breakfast – invariably bacon, egg, etc., then your bread. Then you would sit down at your chosen table. You'd start your breakfast and a sergeant would walk into the dining hall accompanied by the officer of the day and he would say, "Morning, any complaints?" He was a very brave man who stood up and said, "Well sir, I'm not too fond of the porridge....." I cannot remember anybody being brave enough, woe betide you! It was a substantial meal – it wouldn't do for any mummy's boy, it would break your heart. *Dick Fiddament, 105 Squad, Britannia Barracks*

The day would be divided up into sessions across the day and one of the first priorities of the army was to bring the callow young men up to a basic level of physical fitness so that they could actually withstand the greater tests that lay before them in their training.

> You had to do press-ups and they came round to make sure you were in the proper position. Arms shoulder-width apart, posterior in the correct position, no sagging stomachs. Up-down, up-down, up-down – until you thought you were about to collapse – every muscle and every conceivable bone in your body literally throbbed! *Dick Fiddament, 105 Squad, Britannia Barracks*

Prime amongst all the training sessions were those devoted to basic foot and rifle drill on the parade ground.

> You'd be formed up in your squad and you'd be called to attention. Your rifle would be in your right hand and your left hand would be rigid at your side with the thumb in line with the seams of the trousers. Chin in, chest out, hollowed back and looking straight to your front. Never moved, not an eyelid could be batted. He would say, "Slope arms!" You brought the rifle up from the floor across the body onto your left shoulder with your left hand grasping the butt and your left arm horizontal to the ground. You brought the right hand down at the right hand side. That was

Ready for kit inspection, Sir!

called 'the rifle at the slope' position. So that you did it in unison, initially you had to shout out. So when he said "Slope arms" you would say, "One, one-two, one!" You all shouted that out so you got the thing going in unison. When he gave a command the whole squad would move as one. Later on you would count mentally and you did this whatever drill movement you made. *Dick Fiddament, 105 Squad, Britannia Barracks*

The endless drill sessions may have dulled the senses but it tightened discipline. The men gained increasing pride as they developed an ability to forge a living multi-headed hydra on the parade ground which moved its many arms and legs as one.

★★★★

Weapons training began with the .303 Short Lee Enfield rifle – the same basic rifle used by their fathers before them. It was an exceptionally accurate rifle with a reasonable rate of fire in well trained hands. The training was exhaustive and had already encompassed familiarization lectures, sighting practice and .22 range practice before they got a chance to try the real thing.

You got down in the prone position, you had the rifle in your left hand, you'd flop down on to your right hand and ease yourself down. The more often you did it the quicker you did it. Then you had to lie with your upper torso from the waist straight facing the target and your legs apart about two or three feet, to get the balance. You brought the rifle up with your elbows tucked in, the butt tightly into the shoulder. You relaxed until you got the command, "Load!" There'd be a clip of 303, I think there was five bullets in one of these iron clips. You opened the bolt, you put this clip in the top of the magazine and pushed down. The rounds would slide out straight into the magazine. You then pushed a round up the breech and put your safety catch on. The target would come up, the centre of the target was in red, that was the bull's eye, the ring next to it was called an inner, then the next to that was a black circle which was called the magpie, there was another ring, the extreme and that was known as the outer. *Dick Fiddament, 105 Squad, Britannia Barracks*

The mantra hammered into the recruits was simple in theory.

Get the top of the foresight in the centre of the 'U' and in line with the shoulders of the backsight. The sights thus aligned focus the mark. *Arthur Brough, 105 Squad, Britannia Barracks*

If the rifle was gripped properly into the shoulder the recoil was not too bad as they fired their first shots.

You aimed your rifle at the lowest central portion of the target which allows for the kick. If you aim at the centre or the top it

The ·303 Short Magazine Lee Enfield rifle. Exceptionally accurate and capable of a reasonable rate of fire in well trained hands.
IWM MH 7089

16

would kick up. If you did as you were told and gripped your rifle into your shoulder, and pushed your shoulder forward, it was OK, you did feel something, you could liken it to somebody lightly punching you on the shoulder, no more than that. *Dick Fiddament, 105 Squad, Britannia Barracks*

The time honoured supplement to the rifle was the bayonet. Although to some extent made redundant as effective firing ranges inexorably lengthened, it was still of value at close quarters, particularly because of the sheer intimidatory power of a man charging with 18 inches of cold steel at the end of his rifle. As such bayonet training was still an integral part of a recruit's life.

They had a wooden frame with five or six sacks tightly packed with straw. There was a disc which represented the chest area of an enemy and you would be 10-15 feet away. "Squad, Shun! Squad, Fix Bayonets!" You would bring the rifle and bayonet up with the butt approximately hip height on your right hand side, angled up pointing to just under what would be a man of average height's chin. You would walk forward, slowly, then you would get the command when you were about eight or nine feet away, "Charge!" Then you would go berserk, lower the bayonet, growl, really become aggressive, lunge at the target with all your might, thrust in your bayonet – all an act of course – you never, ever thought that you would do this in anger – thank God I never did! *Dick Fiddament, 105 Squad, Britannia Barracks*

The first Bren guns arrived to replace the elderly Lewis guns and it was immediately obvious that they were a great step forward in light machine-gun design.

To see it beside a Lewis gun it was out of this world, it was like something from outer space by comparison. The Lewis gun was so awkward and such a relic. The Bren gun was weaponry at its most modern. The magazine held 30 or 32 rounds, .303 ball the same as the rifle. The magazine had a curve and you just put this on top of the gun, pulled it down, cocked the gun – pulled the bolt back, the safety catch would be applied straight away. It was similar to firing the rifle, lining up the foresight with the backsight. The target would come up and you would fire in bursts of three – a gentle squeeze on the trigger and you'd fire hopefully into the bull. It was a very, very accurate gun once you got the feel of it. *Dick Fiddament, 105 Squad, Britannia Barracks*

Hand grenades had been used with a vengeance in the trench and dugout fighting which typified the First World War. The No. 36 Mills grenade which had been developed was a formidable weapon at short range, especially in enclosed spaces, where its blast and scything fragmentation were deadly. As such it was treated with care in training.

We went out first on level ground with a dummy. We were told how to hold this grenade, how to pull the pin out, and hold it still. Then we'd point our left arm towards the target. We'd lean backwards with the right hand with the grenade in it. On the command we would then throw this grenade. We'd have a target to throw it at. As soon as it left your hand the handle would fly off and release the pin, but, as it was only a dummy, we didn't have to worry about it. Then we'd go down on to the range and the NCO would show us how to throw the first live one. We were standing in these trenches dug so that each man had his own little piece of trench to throw it in, so that if anything happened the next one wouldn't be killed or wounded. The first time you threw the Mills bomb you wonder what's going to happen. *Ernie Farrow, 105 Squad, Britannia Barracks*

The Bren Gun replaced the Lewis Gun as the infantryman's Light Machine Gun.

The camaraderie that sprang up in the training squads was very powerful. Dick Fiddament the town boy and 'Strips' Farrow the country lad formed a lifelong friendship in 105 Squad which endured for over 60 years.

What was his was mine and vice versa. That applied to all the lads. We had little enough, goodness knows financially, but I've seen the cigarette broken in half and shared, the sandwich broken up, it was nothing to see five or six men having a game of cards, sharing a drink out of the same cup. Everything came down to sharing. I suppose I thought more of 'Strips' and my other pals than my own biological brother. You lived together. To sum it up – you're a family. *Dick Fiddament, 105 Squad, Britannia Barracks*

It was a hard life with few comforts and no luxuries. Nevertheless most seem to have accepted the consequences of their decision to enlist with equanimity.

I settled down quite well, I knew I'd signed on for seven years and I said to myself, "You've signed on now, you've got to be there seven years, you've got to take it all – and I did. I just took everything that was coming. *Ernie Farrow, 105 Squad, Britannia Barracks*

Their lives were utterly dominated by 'bull' and repetitive routine training but its justification would only really become apparent in war conditions, when less ingrained forms of behaviour could be swept aside by the horrors of battle. Discipline brought instant obedience and helped avoid hesitation which might be fatal on the battlefield.

The idea of discipline was that when the order comes to stand fast it can be pretty terrifying. Because it does happen sooner or later. Or when you're told to open fire. It's one thing to fire at a target made of paper and wood and its another thing to deliberately fire at something that you know is like you – flesh and blood and bone, who has a family, probably married with young children, a mother and a father. That they are doing what you are doing – because its the policy of your particular government of the time. *Dick Fiddament, 105 Squad, Britannia Barracks*

On finishing their training the squads were assigned to either the 1st or 2nd Battalions of the Royal Norfolk Regiment. The 1st Battalion was in India where, in 1938-9, they were approaching the end of a ten year posting. As such most men were sent to the 2nd Battalion who were on the plum short posting at Gibraltar from March 1937 to January 1939, at which time they returned to a period of intensive training at Bordon near Aldershot.

★★★★

In Europe the rise to power in Germany of Adolf Hitler and the Nazi Party could no longer be ignored. Hitler's expansionist policies were pursued with a total disregard for the conventional realities of diplo-

After the Munich crisis of 1938 it became obvious to most that war was inevitable. Chamberlain arrives in Germany to reason things out with Hitler and avoid another World conflict through compromise. Hitler went on to gamble that Britain would not go to war over his invasion of Poland. Taylor Library

macy but, in the absence of any real opposition at home or abroad, he was startlingly successful as he sought to create a 'Greater' Germany at the centre of Europe. Czechoslovakia and Austria were first swallowed and then Poland was earmarked to suffer from the next lurch to the east of the German border. Weakness and indecision were the underlying hallmarks of the response of the Allies which had fought and defeated Germany and the Central Powers in the First World War at such grievous cost. In truth that cost had been so great that no democratic country was willingly to contemplate a further Armageddon just twenty years after the 'war to end wars'. Lone voices warned of the need to re-arm in the face of Hitler's aggression but it was only after the Munich crisis of 1938 that it became obvious to most that war was inevitable. Britain belatedly began a military expansion and all her existing armed forces began to prepare for war – not as an abstract proposition – but as a grim reality.

I realised that I had joined an infantry regiment. When I joined I didn't realize what the infantry were – that they were the fighting soldiers of the British Army. We were the people that had to do the fighting. All the rest like artillery and Royal Corps of Signals, RASC, RAOC, REME and all the rest – they didn't do the fighting. They were there to support us at the front line to give us everything we needed. We were the boys who met the enemy eye to eye and we would have to do the fighting. There was that apprehension, "What have I done? Why did I join an infantry regiment?" It suddenly sunk into our brains, not only me but other people as well, "What the hell have we let ourselves in for?" *Private Ernie Leggett, HQ Coy, 2nd Norfolks*

At Bordon Camp the returned 2nd Battalion flung themselves into their training with a relish. Every year individual weapons training was supplemented by tactical training at platoon and company levels but in the summer of 1939 there was a renewed urgency. Officers may have been peripheral figures during basic training but in the battalion structure they now came into their own.

> I controlled the company by direct contact. I knew the men individually jolly well and I knew their family background well. I knew which of them were married and this sort of thing. I think they appreciated the fact that one had taken the trouble to find this out. They used to come along with any sort of family problems they'd got. I think this helped to weld the unit into a close knit team which it undoubtedly was. *Captain Peter Barclay, A Coy, 2nd Norfolks*

Barclay threw himself and his men into their tactical training. As war loomed the principles of attacking a defended position were of crucial importance if lives were to be saved.

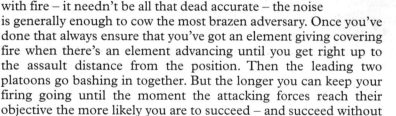

> The first thing is to smother the opposition as much as you can with effective fire. When you've got a demoralized enemy to contend with you're going to capture your objective a lot quicker and with a lot less loss. So the first principle was to shatter their morale with fire – it needn't be all that dead accurate – the noise

Peter Barclay

is generally enough to cow the most brazen adversary. Once you've done that always ensure that you've got an element giving covering fire when there's an element advancing until you get right up to the assault distance from the position. Then the leading two platoons go bashing in together. But the longer you can keep your firing going until the moment the attacking forces reach their objective the more likely you are to succeed – and succeed without heavy loss. *Captain Peter Barclay, A Coy, 2nd Norfolks*

The battalion moved to Oxney Camp in May 1939 and as the international situation spiralled out of control they were mobilized at 16.40 on 1 September.

> I was full of admiration about the way that it was conducted. There was endless documentation about what was to be carried out in the various stages of the proceedings. We had a very efficient

Throughout the British Isles men were being kitted out for the approaching conflict.
Taylor Library

Adjutant, one Major Marshall and it all worked like clockwork.
Every day, everybody knew what had to be done. That went
smoothly. *Captain Peter Barclay, A Coy, 2nd Norfolks*

The Medical Officer and his team began a thorough programme of
health and fitness tests designed to weed out all those regulars who,
whilst perfectly adequate for peacetime service, were simply not up to
the physical stresses of active service in the field. To compensate the

battalion was brought right up to strength by reservists who were called back to the colours from their civilian lives.

Our reservists joined us all over the place and brought us up to strength with a marvellous contingent of trained men, most of whom had only recently left the battalion. They were simply splendid, a very good type of man, by and large, and I heard no adverse repercussions at all. I think a great many were jolly glad to get back! They fitted straight in then because they had been thoroughly trained during the seven years that they'd done with the colours. *Captain Peter Barclay, A Coy, 2nd Norfolks*

The men were more forthright amongst themselves perhaps than in front of a gilded officer. Not all of them wanted to return to army life.

Actually it was a shame really because those people had done their army service, they'd gone back into civvie street, they were living a normal life and they were called back into the army – a lot of them were killed. They didn't react in a bad way, they were pleased to be back with comrades who they knew, we'd served with them. They talked about civilian life and how they were getting on, some of them were happily in work, good jobs – but regardless of what job they were in they had to come back. Some of them had been married, a settled life. Most of them thought it was unfair that they should be called back. We sympathized with them, it was a terrible thing really to be called back. *Private Ernie Leggett, A Coy 2nd Norfolks*

One reservist did not even get the chance of one day at home in his 'civvies' before he was recalled to the colours.

About two nights before the war broke out our Lance Corporal, 'Misler' Mason, had finished his seven years in the regulars and he was waiting to be transferred to the reserve. We all went down to Fleet to celebrate his 'demob' if you like. When we got back, we were all in the same tent as 'Misler' and he'd given all his clothes away that he didn't want – we'd all scrounged different things off him. But in the early morning the orderly sergeant came round, found his tent and said, "'Misler', hand your civvies in and draw your uniforms out!" Everything had been cancelled so poor 'Misler' had to start to be a soldier again. *Ernie Farrow, 2nd Norfolks*

The whole battalion was kitted out in the new 'battledress' style uniforms which had been designed to be more practical in active service conditions.

I liked it because it was easy, you had a pair of trousers with a big pocket on the thigh of each side where you could put your oddments like maps and compasses. Then you had a small jacket that had two pockets at the top. I found it most comfortable,

The Boyes anti–tank rifle.   Taylor Library

probably not as smart but easy to wear. *Private Ernie Leggett, HQ Coy, 2nd Norfolks*

Specialist equipment was issued and the men were introduced to the weapon with which they were to hold back the marauding German panzers – the mighty Boyes anti–tank rifle.

> It was virtually an elephant rifle. We quickly put it through its paces. I fired it myself – it had a kick back like a mule, I can tell you. It fired just a large bullet but it would have penetrated the skin of a three quarter track German vehicle but I think it would bounce off a tank like a pea. *Captain Peter Barclay, A Coy, 2nd Norfolks*

They were also becoming increasingly familiar with the ubiquitous Bren carriers

> The carriers were to get a Bren gun and equipment from one point to another as quick as possible. In other words if you had an open flank on either side that was the Bren gun carriers' job – to go and fill that gap. The Bren would be taken off and the carrier would be taken back a few hundred yards and camouflaged. The driver should have stayed with the carrier but in practice that didn't happen! The sergeant and the gunner would go forward, scrape themselves a little hole facing the enemy. The driver would be ready for any call the NCO made. *Private Herbert Limes, Carrier Platoon, HQ Coy, 2nd Norfolks*

As the thousand and one preparations went whirling by in a welter of

Lord Gort, Commander of the British Expeditionary Force, and his staff arrive in France.   Taylor Library

Quartermaster's sweat and sergeants' curses, the men made a symbolic break with their lives, past and future, as civilians.

As we'd been in the army a certain time we were allowed to wear civilian clothes. But with the outbreak of the war we had to hand it all back in again. So what we did was packed everything that belonged to us personally into a kitbag which we had been issued with. We were given labels and they were sent back to our home addresses to our next of kin. So that was the last time we saw them until after the war. We didn't feel anything about it at all. I don't know whether we were pleased or sorry. We were at war and this was what we'd joined the army for and that was all there was to it. We were going somewhere different and hope to pray that we come back safe again. *Private Ernie Farrow, Pioneer Section, HQ Coy, 2nd Norfolks*

Many would never return.

CHAPTER TWO

The Phoney War

The 2nd Norfolks took their place with the rest of the 2nd Infantry Division in the British Expeditionary Force (BEF). Alongside the 1st Battalion Royal Scots and the 1/8th Battalion Lancashire Fusiliers they formed the 4th Brigade. The BEF had been assigned to defend the Franco/Belgian border abutting the imposing main French defences of the Maginot Line which extended along the Franco/German border. On 21 September the 2nd Norfolks became the first battalion of the BEF to land in France and they were initially billeted in the countryside around the old First World War battlefields at Arras. They received a pleasant enough reception from the French.

Soldiers of the British Expeditionary Force move up to the Front during the Winter of 1939.
Taylor Library

They were very friendly, especially the older people who'd experienced the First World War. And one of the main things in the cafés was they wanted us to sing all the old First World War songs that they knew, 'Pack up Your Troubles', 'Tipperary', 'Keep the home Fires Burning' – they remembered all of them and some could even join in the singing. We had some very good evenings with them. *Signaller R Brown, HQ Coy, 2nd Norfolks*

There were the usual cultural frissons as the men discovered that the French were strangely un-English in the way they lived their lives.

They're terribly conservative of course – the beer wasn't the right sort of beer and the French cooking was too oily or whatever – they really took a long time to get used to anything other than the customary victuals. They didn't touch wine, they didn't take to that at all kindly. Calvados, occasionally, if they were feeling flush. *Captain Peter Barclay, A Coy, 2nd Norfolks*

In this respect Barclay at least partially underestimated his men.

When we got back in the evenings we went to the cafés almost every night. Typically French cafes, the French would drink wine and we started to drink wine as well because there was not much beer. French beer didn't taste like beer, it was a little bit vinegary to me. We started to drink wine and the wine they drank was not the medium sweet which we had been used to at home, it was sort of a bitter wine, but I got used to it and I got a nice habit for it – I started to drink wine all the time, red wine. They drank it and we thought, "Well, if they can drink it, why shouldn't we?" *Private Ernie Leggett, HQ Coy, 2nd Norfolks*

In early October they moved up to the Belgian frontier at the small village of Rumigies. Here the Norfolks were on the extreme right of the British line and they began the onerous task of constructing part of a continuous series of trenches which were to be known as the Gort Line after the BEF Commander in Chief Lieutenant-General Sir John Gort. These defences were intended to act as a continuation of the Maginot Line along the Belgian frontier to the sea. The men found that Belgian ground conditions had not changed since their fathers dug in on the Western Front in 1914-18.

It was a waterlogged area and in some places we couldn't dig deep enough. We tried to go down about six feet but if we could only manage four then we had to build revetments above and make our own wattle hurdles out of wood and fill them with soil and stones to build it above ground. We had pumps going if the trench was any depth to take water out all the while. *Signaller R Brown, HQ Coy, 2nd Norfolks*

The line was not well sited and the problems encountered were overcome with an ingenuity which only highlighted the underlying problems of using a frontier as the basis for a defensive line.

Our job was to prepare defences along the line of a little stream which in some cases meant that there was practically no field of fire at all. Rather than drop back and take up a reverse slope position we had to defend the frontier – presumably because this stream did provide in most places an anti-tank obstacle. Many of my platoon section positions were breastworks and some even were built in trees to raise them off the ground sufficiently to give a field of fire – with of course an enormous 'build up' or foundation underneath. We had to make hurdles, stiffened up by either lopped off trees or great thick stakes and filled with earth. They were quite extraordinary and really, seemingly ridiculous. Enormously high breastworks in front and a splinter proof backdrop behind, otherwise they resembled trenches in trees. Never used in the war at any stage and I should think people were thankful they didn't have to! *Captain Peter Barclay, A Coy, 2nd Norfolks*

Labour Party Leader Clement Attlee and Lord Gort inspect the newly dug British defensive positions. IWM F2058

The battalion was regularly visited during that winter by a variety of curious Generals but Captain Barclay had most cause to recall a visit from Winston Churchill.

He was in tremendous good form. He came along followed by an array of brass. I had a little mongrel and as we were walking along from one position to another she suddenly started barking at a pile of faggots. Winston was most intrigued by this. He said, "A little sport, a little sport?" "Yes, if we play it right!" He said, "Well, let's play it right, how do you want it played?" I said, "What we really want to do is get three officers on top of that pile of faggots and have them bounce – then they'll bolt the rabbit and we'll have a hunt!" His eyes lit up and the three senior generals were ordered on to this pile of faggots, directed by Winston, as orchestra conductor as it were. He synchronized the bouncing.

General Ironsides, Winston Churchill, General Gamelin and General Gort, during Churchill's visit to France in the Winter of 1939-1940. IWM F2092

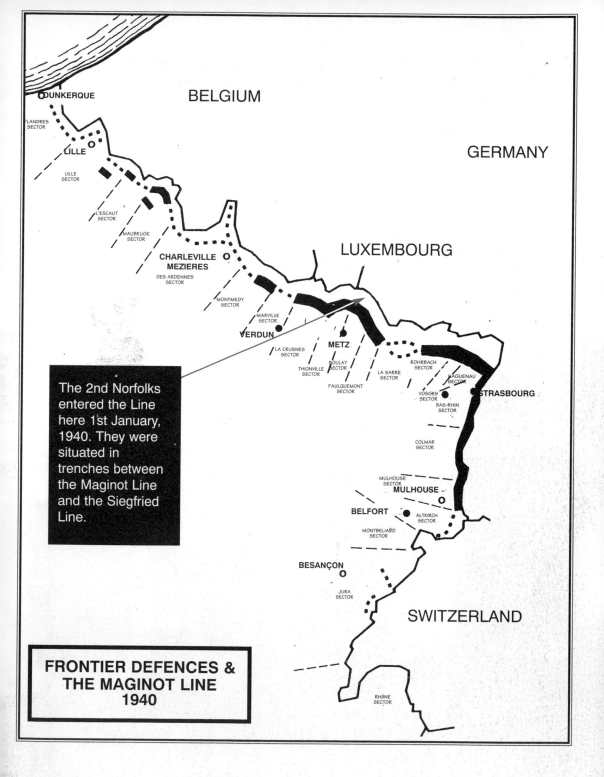

BELGIUM

GERMANY

LUXEMBOURG

DUNKERQUE

FLANDRES
SECTOR

LILLE

LILLE
SECTOR

L'ESCAUT
SECTOR

MAUBEUGE
SECTOR

CHARLEVILLE
MEZIERES

DES ARDENNES
SECTOR

MONTMEDY
SECTOR

MARVILLE
SECTOR

VERDUN

LA CRUSNES
SECTOR

THIONVILLE
SECTOR

METZ

BOULAY
SECTOR

FAULQUEMONT
SECTOR

LA SARRE
SECTOR

ROHRBACH
SECTOR

HAGUENAU
SECTOR

VOSGES
SECTOR

BAS-RHIN
SECTOR

STRASBOURG

COLMAR
SECTOR

MULHOUSE
SECTOR

MULHOUSE

BELFORT

ALTKIRCH
SECTOR

MONTBELIARD
SECTOR

BESANÇON

JURA
SECTOR

SWITZERLAND

RHÔNE
SECTOR

The 2nd Norfolks
entered the Line
here 1st January,
1940. They were
situated in
trenches between
the Maginot Line
and the Siegfried
Line.

**FRONTIER DEFENCES &
THE MAGINOT LINE
1940**

31

They had no alternative, they were just ordered up there by Winston and ordered to bounce. They looked pretty foolish with their ADCs looking on, but they entered into the spirit of the thing. Sure enough, very shortly, the rabbit bolted and we had a most exciting hunt which intrigued Winston no end, when my little dog gave tongue and hurtled after the rabbit. Captain Peter Barclay, A Coy, 2nd Norfolks

On Christmas Day the battalion began a tedious journey for a tour of duty on the left of the Maginot Line. On 1 January 1940 they finally arrived to take up their positions in the *Ligne de Contact* a mile in the front of the village of Walweisstroff on the Saar front.

We were between the Maginot Line and the Siegfried Line and there we came on these trenches. There was hardly anything above the ground – only snow. They were trenches that had been dug down and revetted with duckboards in them. They were all dry because of these frosts which dried everything up. In some places they were dug underground, the company headquarters was underground, but we were on top in the trenches. We just had the stars above us. It was very, very cold and at night-time we got inside our big bags. During the day we managed to find some sandbags that we filled full of straw and wrapped them round our

The Ligne de Contact *trenches in the Maginot Line with British troops facing the Germans in their static positions in front of the Siegfried Line.* IWM F2260

German infantrymen experience the same conditions as their counterparts across No-Man's-Land in the waiting and watching game of the Phoney War. Taylor Library

legs to keep our legs and feet warm, much better to walk about like that as well. One morning looking over the top of the trench in the distance I could see someone moving about. We were told that they were the Germans and to keep our heads down because their snipers were quite apt to pick you off at that distance – so we kept our heads well down after that. *Private Ernie Farrow, Pioneer Section, HQ Coy, 2nd Norfolks*

Sergeant Walter Gilding of the Mortar Platoon took over a dugout from his opposite numbers in the Royal Scots.

The mortar pit had already been dug into the railway embankment and there was a place dug at the back into the bank of the railway. They'd made up a little fire stove place in there with a metal funnel coming out of the top. On arriving there we lit up, but found that we were choking to death with smoke for five days. The day we left I checked outside in the chimney and found it had been stuffed up by some old pair of socks – the Scots had done this as a joke. The detachment commander said, "It's impossible to take the base plate out of the ground its frozen in!" So I just handed over my base plate to him and took over his. When I was relieved I did the same thing – you just couldn't dig it out it was frozen in. We were all fairly young and fit I suppose that makes all the difference – but it was so cold. We huddled together in this little dugout at the back of the mortar pit and I don't think we hardly looked out of it for the five days. We had a sentry at the opening of the pit. I had a pair of binoculars I could look across the railway line to this wood 900 yards away where we'd seen the Germans. Each morning they used to come out with a towel round their necks, where they'd been having a wash and wave it to us. We used to say, "God, why can't we..." We'd got mortar bombs, we were in range. We were ordered not to fire by the battalion headquarters, by the CO. At the time we thought maybe they're discussing peace terms or something of that nature and they didn't want us to provoke the situation. It didn't make sense to us, we were there to fight a war and we weren't allowed to get on with it. *Sergeant Walter Gilding, Mortar Platoon, HQ Coy, 2nd Norfolks*

It was not just the men who were frustrated at not being allowed to do the job for which they had trained for so long.

There were some railway carriages on an embankment which ran through No Mans Land and the Germans used this as an observation post. Occasionally I could see them with a pair of field glasses moving through the carriages. I thought, "Well, that's a jolly good gunner target!" So I ordered fire to be brought down by the French artillery 75s which were supporting us. Nothing happened to my indignation and I got onto Battalion Headquarters to find out why I wasn't receiving the response to which I reckoned I was entitled. They said, "Oh, it's not a legitimate target – the only legitimate target you should know by now is a working party in the open". Such was the 'Phoney War'! *Captain Peter Barclay, A Coy, 2nd Norfolks*

Instead of the fighting they had anticipated, and perhaps inwardly dreaded, they were once again working to improve lines of defences.

We had this Dannett wire, round rings of wire. This came up, lorry loads of it. We had to get this out at night in the dark in certain positions. We took an iron stake out with us and tried to drive it into the ground. The ground was frozen stiff. Because we couldn't get it in very far we had a rope and two of us would stand back with this rope on top of the post to hold it back . Then they'd pull this Dannett wire out, hundreds of yards of it and make it fast at the other end. Then we'd find a small stake to drive into the ground again to hold the damned thing up straight which was a heck of a job. *Private Ernie Farrow, Pioneer Section, HQ Coy, 2nd Norfolks*

Intelligence was prized by the higher authorities on both sides and night patrols were sent out to probe across the 800-1000 yards of No Mans Land to determine the exact nature of the opposing defences. On 4 January, two British patrols were sent out. One, commanded by Lieutenant Everitt, returned without incident, although they were able to claim the honour of being the first British patrol to cross the German border in the war. The other, under Captain Peter Barclay, encountered trouble as he penetrated the German lines around Waldwisse railway station.

Peter Barclay carefully planning that night's patrol (Reconstruction).   IWM F2268

They wanted to know what sort of set up there was the other side of the enormously elaborate barbed wire entanglement that the Germans had in front of their positions and a prisoner was wanted for identification purposes. So I went out with a patrol of five, one other officer and three chaps. We were out most of the night. I suppose it took about an hour-and-a-half to get up to their positions. The first positions we came to were empty. They had built up breastworks, I suppose because the ground was so hard and that combined with a better field of fire. They had a most lavish display of barbed wire entanglements in front of their positions but luckily we could see where to get through because there were tracks in the snow. Every now and then we had to do a bit of cutting to get through. We went a long way into the German position and discovered a great deal of information – we didn't get a prisoner. It was a moonlit night and of course the clouds were there to help you one minute and gone the next. There was a house which they'd been using a very short time before we got

The patrol sets out into No Man's Land with Captain Peter Barclay in the lead (Reconstruction).
IWM F2274

there. But after casing the joint they'd obviously moved to other positions. As I came out of this house we were spotted and a grenade landed between my legs, a light egg- Bakelite - grenade. It damaged my boots but didn't damage me! We came under a very heavy fire from all over the place but luckily it was inaccurate and we all managed to make our way home. *Captain Peter Barclay, A Coy, 2nd Norfolks*

For this piece of daring Captain Peter Barclay was awarded the Military Cross – the first BEF officer to be decorated in the war, whilst Lance

Peter Barclay and his reconnaissance patrol checking possible German outposts (Reconstruction).

IWM F2273

Captain Barclay and Corporal Davies receiving congratulations from the men after being awarded their medals. IWM F2200

Corporal H Davis received the Military Medal. Unfortunately his exploits seems to have heightened the attentiveness of German sentries. On 7 January 1940 Lieutenant Everitt took out another patrol and a more melancholy 'first' was recorded.

Lieutenant Everitt took a patrol out from our lads. I had a very bad cough and every five minutes I was coughing, so he said, "Oh, you'd better stop behind, I'm not taking you because you'll give the game away, you'll give our positions away!" He gave me some acid sweets that he'd had sent from England, he said, "Here, you have them, they'll cure your cough, you do the cooking for the lads whilst we're away and when we come back we want our cup of tea and a sandwich!" I said, "OK, Sir, that'll be alright!" The next thing the Sergeant came running back, he'd got shot through the arm, a couple more lads were shook up, I said, "What's happening? What's happening?" They said, "Lieutenant Everitt's just been shot out of a tree, we've had to leave him and run!" He was the first British officer to be killed in France and they gave him a military funeral with flags and everything. *Private William Cron, Carrier Platoon, HQ Coy, 2nd Norfolks*

The battalion took its turn in both the Ligne de Contact and the reserve Ligne de Recule. These lines were really just outer defences to the Maginot Line itself – the Ligne de Resistance.

It was absolutely unbelievable. It was controlled like a hub of a battleship. There was an enormous office with press buttons and switches all over the place deep down in the bowels of one of these forts. When a mortar, for instance, was called upon to fire, a button was pressed and a cupola on top of the tower rose up. This fired and then having been fired it was lowered down again. It was mechanized to the nth degree. *Captain Peter Barclay, A Coy, 2nd Norfolks*

However many of the Norfolks, officers and men were worried by the supine attitude of the French garrison.

They had a motto, "On ne passe pas" which applied basically to the Maginot Line. All the French soldiers and a lot of the French population had little badges with a fortress and 'On ne passe pas' stamped across it. This had an adverse effect in fact on the French Army as a whole. They had a totally passive attitude to the war; an indoctrination of being ready to receive rather than to go on the offensive. They were firmly of the opinion that the Maginot Line couldn't be crossed anywhere and that as long as they sat on that and used the enormous fire power it was capable of producing, they could keep the Germans on the other side. They were dead against any form of patrolling and they just sat in their trenches all through the night and waited for anything to happen that might happen. *Captain Peter Barclay, A Coy, 2nd Norfolks*

At the end of their month's tour of duty the Norfolks returned to Rumigies before being assigned to the Divisional Reserve based at Orchies. Here life was made up of digging yet another set of trenches, training, sports and, best of all, home leave. The battalion had attracted considerable press interest due to the mini-dramas of the Saar night patrols. These inherently trivial affairs were blown out of all proportion by pressmen desperate for hard news in the tedium of the 'Phoney War'.

Press photographers invaded in large numbers and the patrol had to re-enact its exploits in front of a News Cameraman; fortunately snow was still on the ground! The rum issue before the patrol set out was of intense interest to the cameraman and had to be re-enacted until he was quite satisfied as to its efficiency, a proceeding more than satisfying to the patrol! *Captain William Murray-Brown, 2nd Norfolks*

By the Spring the officers were aware of the existence of the unpromisingly named 'Plan D'. In the event of a German offensive, this envisaged the immediate movement of the BEF across Belgium to take up positions on the River Dyle. The Norfolks were to take up advanced positions at Wavre some 25 miles south east of Brussels. Normal reconnaissance was impossible so the Norfolk's officers bent the 'rules' to achieve their goal.

It was an extraordinary performance because we weren't supposed to go in uniform and so mufti had to be sent out for us. We all went in mufti suits by car across to the eastern Belgium frontier. There on the ground, we reconnoitred the positions we were to take in the event of the Germans attacking from that angle. We knew exactly where to go and what positions to dig as soon as we arrived there. *Captain Peter Barclay, A Coy, 2nd Norfolks*

The 'Phoney War' was about to end. On the 9 April news was received of the German invasion of Denmark and Norway. As a result on 11 April the Norfolks were placed on six hours' notice to be ready for the advance to the Dyle should the Germans invade Belgium.

We didn't know much about Norway at all. We had our own little goings on where we were and we hardly knew what was going on anywhere else in the world – only around Orchies. *Private Ernie Farrow, Pioneer Section, HQ Coy, 2nd Norfolks*

A guard of honour for French General Georges supplied by men of the 2nd Battalion The Royal Norfolk Regiment. The period known as the 'Phoney War' was about to come to an end.

CHAPTER THREE

The Road to Le Paradis

The real war burst with awe-inspiring force on 10 May 1940 when the Germans tore up the 'rule book' and launched a pile driving offensive, by-passing the Maginot Line completely, tearing ferociously through neutral Luxembourg and Belgium. In accordance with 'Plan D' the BEF immediately moved forward to meet them on the Dyle. The Norfolks packed up their kit in double quick time and moved off to a concentration area at the Forêt de Marchinne. Here Ernie Leggett, who had recently been posted to A Company, had an early experience of one of the minor horrors of war.

The field kitchens came out and we were fed and that's where what we called the 'hard tack' came into being. Hard biscuits that you couldn't eat because it took the roof of your mouth away. They had to be soaked in water, then added to bully beef and there was

German infantrymen caught by the propaganda cameraman entering Belgian territory on the morning of 10 May 1940.   Taylor Library

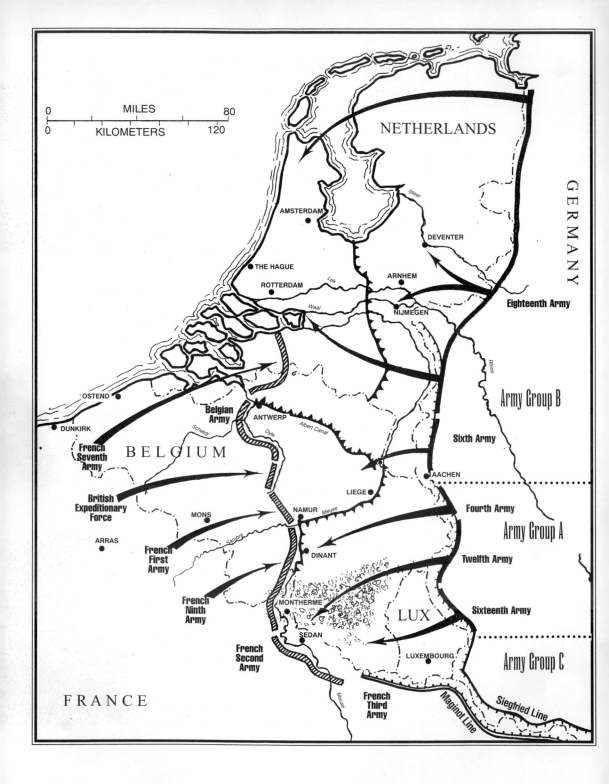

MILES
0 80
0 120
KILOMETERS

GERMANY

NETHERLANDS

AMSTERDAM

DEVENTER

Ijssel

THE HAGUE

ARNHEM

ROTTERDAM

Lek

NIJMEGEN

Waal

Eighteenth Army

Rhine

Army Group B

OSTEND

Belgian
Army

ANTWERP

Albert Canal

DUNKIRK

Sixth Army

French
Seventh
Army

BELGIUM

Scheldt

Dyle

AACHEN

British
Expeditionary
Force

MONS

NAMUR

LIEGE

Fourth Army

Army Group A

Meuse

ARRAS

Sambre

French
First
Army

DINANT

Twelfth Army

French
Ninth
Army

MONTHERME

LUX

Sixteenth Army

Army Group C

SEDAN

LUXEMBOURG

French
Second
Army

Meuse

French
Third
Army

Maginot Line

Siegfried Line

FRANCE

42

a sort of a big mash made with cans of beans and everything. We all had a mess tin and you ate this stuff with your spoon. It was just a horrible mess really. But it filled you. *Private Ernie Leggett, A Coy 2nd Norfolks*

The men were perhaps a little edgy as they marched off to the 'Real War'. Their officers and senior NCOs sought to brief their troops and pass on some last words of advice.

When darkness had fallen Captain Barclay, Sergeant Major Gristock and some of the sergeants came out carrying a hurricane lamp. He said, "Right ho, lads, gather round, I've got something to tell you! We are now at war. As we were marching along you saw the bombers come over, you heard what happened to Orchies where we've just come from, they tried to bomb us but fortunately we're here – we beat them!" He gave us a

Ernie Legget

fatherly talk. The last words he said were, "Now more than ever before, will your training stand you in good stead, keep your heads down and spirits high, and from now on when you aim your rifle to shoot, you shoot to kill!" They were ominous words. He then said, "The best of luck men!" After that we just formed up and marched away into the darkness. *Private Ernie Leggett, A Coy 2nd Norfolks*

The main body of the battalion moved off at 01.30 on 11 May.

The journey was uneventful though rather nerve racking because we had been warned that we would inevitably be bombed and machine gunned during our entry into Belgium. However the inevitable for some unaccountable reason did not happen. It was at Taelaevon where we debussed that we had our first experience of bombing. Just as we were debussing a Heinkel flew over us at about 7,000 feet. Some mad fool started firing a Bren gun at it. Within a few minutes every gun in the convoy was firing at it regardless of the fact that it was miles out of range. *Second Lieutenant D E Jones, D Coy, 2nd Norfolks*

In the excitement of the moment the men seized on their chance to express their martial ardour.

It was very, very high really, there was not a hope in hell of hitting it with a Bren gun from that distance. Three or four pieces came from that aircraft and cries went up that they'd hit it! Of course they hadn't hit it at all – they were four bombs they were dropping! They splattered all around us! *Private Herbert Limes, Carrier Platoon, HQ Coy, 2nd Norfolks*

The result was that the Heinkel having unloaded its bombs, luckily without doing any damage, flew off to let its friends

Herbert Limes

know what was happening. The consequence was inevitable and very soon the Norfolks became aware for the first time of the terrifying power of the Stuka dive bombers as they screamed down on the column.

It wasn't only the bombs and the machine guns that was frightening but they all had this siren attached to them. When they dive bombed you this noise went right through your brain. Much worse than the bombs and the machine guns. We tried to put our fingers in our ears to stop the noise getting through. *Private Ernie Farrow, Pioneer Section, HQ Coy, 2nd Norfolks*

The battalion took up their defensive posts as the advance guard on the south bank of the River Dyle in the Bois de Tombeek.

The position was a good one. The river was a good Anti-Tank obstacle, it was well wired and there were several very good Belgian Pill Boxes and semi-dug trenches. *Second Lieutenant D E Jones, D Coy, 2nd Norfolks*

Captain Barclay and A Company were given the honour of performing the vital outpost role across the Dyle and several miles west of the main line.

My orders basically, in brief, were, "Give 'em a bloody nose, old boy, and then pull out!" There was a small chateau in the area of my company position and a garden party going on. There was a May pole with children whirling round and Madame exercising her role as hostess superbly. She was horrified when I told her we were going to have to dig trenches in and around her garden. She said, "As long as you don't upset the rosebushes and don't interfere with the rhododendrons, I suppose I can't stop you!" Anyhow the party went on and we dug our trenches in amongst it all. I had slit trench positions based on the platoon, two platoons up and one platoon back. They had a very good field of fire from jolly good concealed positions which we were able to prepare quite quickly and camouflage over – a vital finale. *Captain Peter Barclay, A Coy, 2nd Norfolks*

The signs that disaster had befallen the Belgian Army were fairly clear throughout 12 May. Bedraggled and clearly demoralized Belgian soldiers fell back through Barclay's outpost line, at first just a few, but later in increasing numbers. Civilian refugees began to flood back against a soundscape of the ever increasing thunder of German artillery. Finally the Germans appeared.

The vanguard of their advance guard consisted of motorbikes and sidecars with machine guns mounted on the sidecars. We let them get jolly close because we wanted to get as many as we could. I think the leading one was only about 150 yards away. We knocked out about four or five of these and in fact none of the first batch got back to report. But it obviously didn't take long before

The German 'sharp end' in their phenomenal advance – the motorcycle combinations. Here a motorcycle unit forges ahead in the French countryside passing the Headquarter's Group of the 7th Panzer Division.　　　　　　　　　　　　　　　　IWM RML298

the follow up troops smelt a rat and we were subjected to a great deal of heavy mortar and artillery fire. We were there about four or five hours, then darkness fell and we had orders to pull out and cover the bridge blowing party after we'd crossed over. *Captain Peter Barclay, A Coy, 2nd Norfolks*

As the Germans built up their strength it was obvious that all the bridges across the Dyle would have to be blown.

The 7th Panzer Division races cross-country. In the foreground is a Czech built Pz Kpfw 38(t), the most numerous of the light tanks employed by the Wehrmacht at the outbreak of war. It was equipped with a 37mm cannon and two 7.92 mgs.　　　　　　IWM RML132

The Royal Engineers were the people who mined nearly all the bridges but we were told that they hadn't mined this particular bridge. Therefore it was the pioneers' duty to go out and do this job. We took our gun cotton with us. We wanted to blast this particular joint on each side of the bridge. This would cause the bridge to fall down. The gun cotton you can tie on with a piece of string, we tied it round and around the best way we could. It was as simple as that. You put the primer and the detonator in. We had an electric wire and batteries so we ran our wire back about two or three hundred yards back from the bridge. The man who was in charge would have the battery in his pocket or in his haversack – no one else would touch that. This was done by Lance Corporal Mason who was in charge of our section at the time. A pair of wires down one side, a pair of wires on the other directly to where he was, they'd then be attached together and at the point when we'd got to blow it up he'd just touch it on the small battery. We didn't get shot at so they couldn't have seen what we were doing. This was a risk that we took. While we were doing this the artillery had orders to cover us more or less. So whenever there was a tank approaching the bridge the artillery blasted them. After we'd left Lance Corporal Mason blew the bridge. We weren't there, he was on his own. We heard the explosion and he came back and reported that the bridge was gone. *Private Ernie Farrow, Pioneer Section, HQ Coy, 2nd Norfolks*

The Norfolks were moved back into divisional reserve and took up new positions behind the Bois de Beaumont above the village of Wavre on 12 May. By the 14 May it was obvious that the Belgian Army was doomed and it was hoped that the Dyle Line would prove the rock which broke the power of the German attack. The BEF settled down for a prolonged defensive action as on 15 May several serious attacks were launched along the whole of the Dyle front. At this stage the Norfolks were confident of the BEF's continuing ability to hold the Dyle line. They were therefore astonished when late on 15 May orders came through to withdraw to take up positions in front of Overyssche. The reason was the tremendous success of the German blitzkrieg attack further south which had smashed through the French lines on the Meuse between Namur and Sedan and was already sweeping round behind the British lines and separating them from the remaining French forces. In these circumstances the tactics of rapid withdrawal were to become sadly familiar to all over the next few days as BEF began to retreat back towards the French frontier.

We never, ever carried out a withdrawal 'in contact'. If we thought that was likely we patrolled very offensively against enemy positions before we pulled out – gave them something to think

Fleeing civilian refugee columns were deliberately targeted by the Stukas so that the roads became clogged and difficult to travel for the Allied troops. Taylor Library

about and then extricated ourselves without fear of interference. We never once were molested in our withdrawal which I was thankful about because nearly always I was a rearguard company and you had a horrible sort of feeling of getting one in the pants as you were coming out. *Captain Peter Barclay, A Coy, 2nd Norfolks*

The roads they had advanced up in such high spirits just a few days before were marked by the evidence of defeat.

There was lines and lines of these poor old people with prams, wheel-barrows, horse and carts. Some with a cow, some with a couple of pigs – trying to drive these down the road. You can just imagine, with our big lorries coming down the Belgian roads which are only narrow, what a problem we had. *Private Ernie Farrow, Pioneer Section, HQ Coy, 2nd Norfolks*

The situation was bad enough but the Luftwaffe sought to smash the fighting strength of the BEF in any way it could. Their tactics were logical but brutal in the extreme.

As soon as we started to withdraw again three of the Stukas came over. Now they took no notice of us, we dived out of the lorries because we expected them to blow us to hell. But they didn't, they simply went over the top of us and disappeared in the trees. We heard the machine guns, we heard the sirens, we heard the bombs dropping. Now on our left flank we had the Belgian Army and we naturally thought that they'd gone after them. But, after we'd driven down the road three or four miles, we found what they'd done. They'd come over us, left us. But to stop us, they'd machine gunned and bombed these poor refugees. This was a massacre. All along the road were people who had been

47

killed, with no arms, no heads, there was cattle lying about dead, there was little tiny children, there was old people. Not one or two people but hundreds of them lying about in the road. This was absolutely a massacre. We couldn't stop to clear the road, because we knew that this is what it was done for – to make us to stop and the Germans would have surrounded us. So we had to drive our lorries over the top of them. Which was heartbreaking – really heartbreaking – for us but we couldn't do anything about it. *Private Ernie Farrow, Pioneer Section, HQ Coy, 2nd Norfolks*

The evidence of the sheer destruction of modern war was everywhere.

The devastation of the villages and towns we walked through – they had just been brought to the ground. There was water and smoke, fires in the streets. I can still remember that terrible smell of death after a bombing or shelling had occurred. People were in these houses, they hadn't been taken out and there was still that horrible stench which we had to go through. Of course there was desolation everywhere. As we went past some woods all the trees had been uprooted, the tops had been shelled away, it was just like walking through a hell. *Private Ernie Leggett, A Coy 2nd Norfolks*

As the retreat went on lack of sleep took its toll and the men were utterly

Aerial attacks were made against villages and towns in front of the German advance ensuring maximum misery for civilians caught up in the malestrom of modern warfare.

IWM F4517

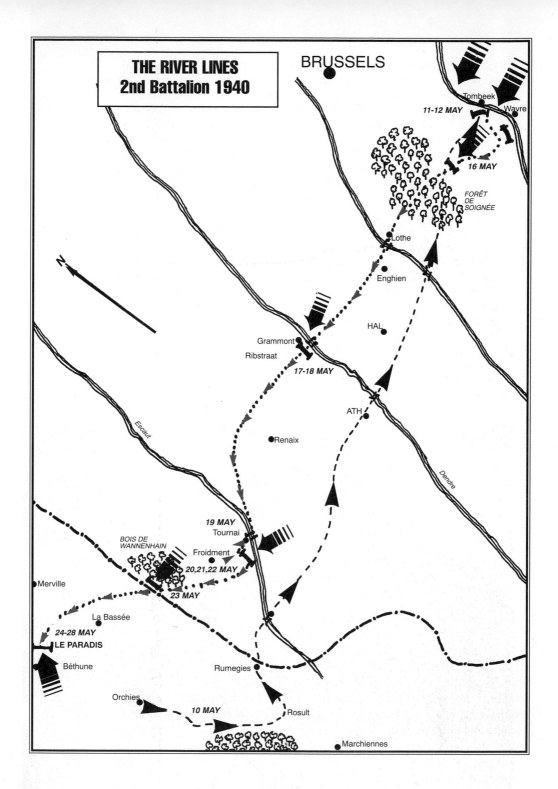

THE RIVER LINES
2nd Battalion 1940

BRUSSELS

Tombeek

Wavre

11-12 MAY

16 MAY

FORÊT DE SOIGNÉE

Lothe

Enghien

HAL

Grammont

Ribstraat

17-18 MAY

ATH

Renaix

Escaut

Dendre

19 MAY

Tournai

BOIS DE WANNENHAIN

Froidment

20,21,22 MAY

Merville

23 MAY

La Bassée

24-28 MAY
LE PARADIS

Béthune

Rumegies

Orchies

10 MAY

Rosult

Marchiennes

N

49

French civilians fleeing from their homes and for their lives at the height of the the German Blitzkrieg. IWM F4514

shattered.

> We marched 25-30 miles in the darkness. People say that you can't march while you're asleep – well I can tell you here and now you can march while you're asleep because I've done it – and all my company did it! The only time you wake up is when you bump into the man ahead of you or the man behind you bumps into you. Marching along asleep in the darkness. *Private Ernie Leggett, A Coy 2nd Norfolks*

The combination of stress and physical exhaustion took its toll on the older officers and it was all too understandable when Colonel De Wilton fell ill and had to be invalided home on 17 May. He was replaced by his second in command, Major Charlton. Still the Norfolks continued to fall back until the late evening of 20 May when they were ordered to make a stand along the Escaut Canal.

We took over from a battalion of The Royal Berkshire Regiment and strengthened and improved the positions during the course of the night. These were on a fairly wide front, the battalion had a very long front to contend with and so of course my company front was also long, about 700 or 800 yards – which was a lot for a company in close country. There were buildings on our side of the canal and there was a plantation on the enemy side so we had to have a pretty effective system of cross fire. My company preparations were completed during the hours of darkness. I went round and they were jolly well camouflaged too. Some were in the cellars with sort of loopholes just under the roofs, one lot hiding behind a garden wall with loopholes – well concealed positions which gave good cover of the frontage I was responsible for. *Captain Peter Barclay, A Coy, 2nd Norfolks*

A Company was in the centre, with D Company on the left and B Company on the right. C Company was placed in reserve. The position had some natural strength, protected as they were from the tanks by the canal, and the bridges had been blown. Nevertheless the troops were far too thinly spread out to withstand any kind of sustained attack.

My section took over a building which presumably had been an old cement factory. The roof was off it but we were able to get up on a veranda on the second floor, fairly high. We got what wood and material we could. We just shoved it up so that we were covered to a certain extent. We were very much concealed. *Private Ernie Leggett, A Coy 2nd Norfolks*

As morning broke on the 21 May, having satisfied himself of the thoroughness his company's defensive preparations, Barclay demonstrated an impressive sang froid.

My batman reported that he'd seen some black rabbits in the park of a chateau in the grounds of which some of my positions were. Not only that but he'd found some ferrets and retrievers shut up in the stables. So we thought we'd get in a bit of sport before the fun began. I had a shotgun with me and we popped these ferrets down a big warren. We were having a rare bit of sport as rabbits bolted out of these burrows when, after about an-hour-and a-half, the shelling started along the river line generally. We came in for a certain amount of this and we thought, "Well we'd better pack in and deal with the other situation!" So back we went to Company Headquarters. *Captain Peter Barclay, A Coy, 2nd Norfolks*

Here he turned his attention to a far more dangerous prey.

After a few more hours the Germans appeared on the far bank. They were totally oblivious of our presence in the immediate vicinity. I told my soldiers on no account to fire until they heard my hunting horn. A German officer appeared and got his map out and appeared to be holding an 'O' Group with his senior warrant officers. Then they withdrew into the wood and we heard a lot of chopping going on and saw the tops of trees flattening out. What they were doing was cutting down young trees to make a long series of hurdles to lay over the top of the blitzed bridge which was in the middle of my sector. Eventually they emerged from this plantation with a number of long hurdles and they proceeded to lay these across the rubble and remains of concrete blocks in the canal. We kept quiet and they still had no idea we were there. I reckoned we'd wait until there were as many as we could contend with on our side of the canal before opening fire. There were SS with black helmets and they started to come across and were standing around in little groups waiting. When we'd enough, about 25, I blew my hunting horn. Then of course all the soldiers opened fire with consummate accuracy and disposed of all the enemy personnel on our side of the canal and also the ones on the bank at the far side – which brought the hostile proceedings to an abrupt halt. *Captain Peter Barclay, A Coy, 2nd Norfolks*

Once the Norfolks had revealed themselves, the Germans retaliated hard. Before they committed any more troops to the attack they sought to stand back and use their superior fire power to materially weaken the defences.

Then of course we came in for an inordinate amount of shelling and mortar fire. After the initial burst of fire and their enormous casualties they knew pretty well where we were. Their mortar fire was very accurate. Not so long after I was wounded in the guts, back and arm. I had a field dressing put on each of my wounds. We'd had several casualties and all the stretchers were out. My batman, with great presence of mind, ripped a door off its hinges and, in spite of my orders to the contrary, tied me to this door. He wouldn't take any orders from me from then – except to go where I told him to go. There I was, tied to this door and I said, "Right, well now you've got to take me round on this door, you've not only got my weight to contend with but the door as well!" Of course that took four people and they took me round to deal with a very threatening situation. *Captain Peter Barclay, A Coy, 2nd Norfolks*

The threat came from a party of Germans which had managed to cross the canal and establish themselves on Barclay's right flank.

Suddenly we were fired on by Germans from our side of the canal. So I had to deplete my small reserve to deal with this. I put my Sergeant Major Gristock in charge of this small force which was about ten men including a wireless operator, a company clerk and various other personnel from Company Headquarters. They were not only to hold my right flank, but deal with a German post that had established itself not very far off on my right. He placed some of his men in position to curtail the activities of the post so effectively that they wiped them out. While this was going on fire came from another German post on our side of the canal. Gristock spotted where this was and he left two men to give him covering fire. He went forward with a Tommy gun and grenades to dispose of this party which was in position behind a pile of stones on the bank of the canal itself. When he was about 20-30 yards from this position, which hadn't seen him, he was spotted by another machine-gun post on the enemy side of the canal. They opened fire on him and raked him through – smashed both his knees. In spite of this he dragged himself till he was within grenade lobbing range, then lay on his side and lobbed the grenade over the top of this pile of stones, belted the three Germans, turned over, opened fire with his Tommy gun and dealt with the lot of them. So in fact with that heroic display of his and the good work done by the rest of that tiny little party, the two enemy groups that crossed the canal were

Sergeant Major George Gristock VC

disposed of. Then the reserve company of my own battalion came up and made good the right flank. Then I think I passed out.
Captain Peter Barclay, A Coy, 2nd Norfolks

Barclay and Gristock were both evacuated with severe wounds. Behind them the fighting raged on and the Norfolks seemed to be holding their own, although at high cost.

We saw the Germans coming at us through the wood and they also had light tanks. We let them have all we'd got, firing the Bren, rifles and everything. I was on the Bren gun firing from the cover of these old benches, tables and God knows what on this veranda. We killed a lot of Germans. They came almost up as far as the river and we really gave them hell and they retreated. They attacked us again and the tanks were coming over their own dead men – to us that was repulsive and we couldn't understand why they did that. We put them back again, we just fired at them, they weren't the heavy tanks. There was no bridge near me so they couldn't get across the river. We managed to keep them on their side, they attacked us three times and three times we sent them back. We were being shelled by their artillery but the mortars were the things which were causing the damage. It was terrible, just terrible, you can more or less hear the thing sort of pump off and the next thing you know there's an explosion. Out of my section in the end there was myself, two other privates and a lance corporal. *Private Ernie Leggett, A Coy 2nd Norfolks*

There then fell one of the strange lulls which occur even in the most tumultuous of battles. All along the battalion frontage the surviving officers and NCOs sought to check their flanks for German interlopers.

The Lance Corporal said to me, "Ernie, nip across see if the bastards are penetrating on our left flank". I left my rifle and I walked across the floor of this second storey building. The next thing I knew, I'd hit the ceiling, then I heard a loud bang. I then came down and hit the floor. I realized that I'd been hit – it was one of those blasted mortars, we'd got no roof, it had come down, hit the concrete floor and that was it – I'd been hit. My left leg was absolutely numb, I was bleeding all over the place, my back was numb from the waist downwards, I couldn't move my legs and all I saw was the blood coming round on the floor. *Private Ernie Leggett, A Coy 2nd Norfolks*

Leggett had multiple minor wounds but the most serious was inflicted by a solid piece of shrapnel, about three-and-a-half inches long by an inch and a half wide, which had ripped through his left buttock and exited via his groin, tearing a huge hole that was gaping wide and spilling out his life's blood.

My pals, they got their, and my, field dressings, we only had one each. It was no good just tying them round, it was insufficient. So they bunged one into the wound at the back, pushed it up, put another one into the wound at the front and they tied the other two on the outside. Then they got a piece of rope and tied a tourniquet. I was bleeding a lot. Fortunately I was numb – I had no pain – that's the amazing thing about it. I just thought of my home and family and what they were going to do when they heard the news. Things like that go through your mind. *Private Ernie Leggett, A Coy, 2nd Norfolks*

They carried him downstairs, dragged him out and then returned, as they must, to their posts. Leggett was left alone to crawl alongside the railway line towards the company headquarters.

I crawled and crawled, they'd taken my trousers off, all I'd got was a rough old pair of pants and battledress top. Meantime they were bombing from above. I was being covered with earth, everything and God knows what... As I was crawling along I was conscious that my finger nails had been worn down so that they were bleeding, my hands were bleeding, pulling myself along. It was determination to get away, like a wounded animal. It took me ages, it was about 100, 120 yards away from our headquarters. I was almost at my last gasp and there was one hell of a big explosion and I was covered with earth and I said, "Please, God help me...." I don't know how long I was out but I then remember my hands and arms being tugged and I heard someone say, "Bloody hell, it's Ernie!" I looked up into the faces of two bandsmen, they take the job of stretcher bearers, Lance Corporal John Woodrow and a chap named 'Bunt' Bloxham. They pulled me out and I heard them talking, "Bloody hell, he's had it!" *Private Ernie Leggett, A Coy 2nd Norfolks*

Captain Barclay and his Company Sergeant Major Gristock had also been taken to the Regimental Aid Post.

The next thing I remember I was in the First Aid Post with my Company Sergeant Major who was in a very bad state. But not too bad to appreciate some jellified brandy pills we were both given and that cheered him up no end. They were delicious and very, very welcome. I was evacuated from the Regimental Aid Post to a larger medical rendezvous. I had a little dog who wouldn't leave me – a darling little black mongrel – and she was lying on the top of me preventing anybody getting near me. Then they cut off my trousers and my little dog was so concerned that they had to put a bag over her and take her away. I never saw her any more – it was too awful. *Captain Peter Barclay, A Coy, 2nd Norfolks*

Here we have, perfectly exemplified, the tragedy, the bathos, the differing scales of suffering that were experienced in war.

Meanwhile behind them the Norfolks fought on and the situation was stabilised by the end of the day. Major Charlton the acting CO had been evacuated wounded and Major Lisle Ryder took over in his stead. Overnight sporadic firing disturbed anybody cool enough to contemplate sleeping and the next day brought no relief as the German mortars and snipers continued to pick away at the dwindling strength of the battalion. Nevertheless the Norfolks held until at midnight on 22 May they received orders to pull back to the Gort Line. The disengagement was carried out smoothly and they retreated, hampered as before by the teeming refugees. The battalion was placed in divisional reserve but any thoughts of rest were cruelly dashed. They were ordered almost immediately to take up positions along the La Bassée Canal in front of the village of Le Paradis where they had to face the German panzer divisions that had swept round to the west of the BEF and threatened to cut off their line of retreat to the Channel Ports. The Norfolks were to hold the line as long as possible to buy time for the BEF to evacuate from Dunkirk. On the early morning of 25 May they arrived and the tired veterans of just 15 days that already seemed an eternity, prepared their slit trenches for one final stand. Ironically they were facing west – the opposite way to the lines held by their fathers on the Western Front in 1914-18.

CHAPTER FOUR

The Massacre

By the time that the 2nd Norfolks reached Le Paradis the multiple confusions and exhaustion of the long fighting retreat were beginning to take effect. Thus, although by the morning of 25 May, A and C Companies were correctly in position along the La Bassée Canal between the Bois Pacqueaut and the Béthune bridge it was found that B and D Companies had gone astray. When they were finally tracked down it was discovered that they had inadvertently taken up positions in a subsidiary loop of the canal. This naturally left a huge gap in the Norfolks' defensive line and in desperation the Pioneer section was ordered to fill the gap between A and C Companies.

We had to go in between two different companies – just the Pioneers which was about twenty of us because we'd lost about eight men by this time. What they told us to do was to go up on to the top of this canal bank and make sure that every round that we fired got a German. We were getting short of ammunition and we must try and make every round count. I was using my .303 rifle, occasionally we took turns in firing the Bren gun but there again we had to be very careful. We found that by using the rifles we could save quite a lot of ammunition. We could pick a German off with our rifle just as well as we could do with the Bren gun where you'd fire probably twenty rounds to hit the same German. After we'd fired a certain amount of rounds, we'd got to scramble back down the bank of the canal, run along a bit, then go up top again – just to try and bluff the Germans that there was a great company of us there. We were being hard pressed, we were being machine gunned, mortared, shelled. We were led to believe that the German tanks were made of cardboard and plywood but by God we knew the difference when they started firing at us – we got our heads down very, very quickly! The most terrible thing that I've ever experienced. We were dug in our little fox holes and we'd keep our heads down but you couldn't be there all the time – you had to get up to fire at the Germans on the other side because those Germans were trying to get across the canal to get at us! The more we were hiding up the less chance we had of stopping them. So we had to go out and fire at them. They were even driving their lorries into the canal and trying to drive their tanks across on these lorries. But the artillery managed to keep them at bay. I don't think we saw an aircraft over our sector at the time.

It was a very frightening thing. It really showed you what war was like. *Private Ernie Farrow, Pioneer Section, HQ Coy, 2nd Norfolks*

The casualties slowly mounted as spinning bullets and scything mortar bomb fragments took their toll. Yet despite constant alarums on both flanks every German attack was countered and against all the odds the line held until the evening when the errant B and D Companies finally moved into the correct positions. The battalion headquarters were by this time located at Druries Farm just outside the village of Le Paradis on the right flank of the position.

It was flat and farmland. From Druries Farm which was battalion headquarters you could see the village with the church about half a mile across country and a few hedgerows, ditches and small trees. All four companies were involved, there was no reserve at all because we were depleted in numbers – so they had to put everybody we had into the defence. *Signaller R Brown, HQ Coy, 2nd Norfolks*

Farrow and the survivors of the Pioneer Section rejoined the Headquarters Company at Druries Farm some time on the evening of 25 May.

I ran into this cow-shed and I was amazed to see all my comrades lying about, some of them had lost a foot, some an arm, they were laying about everywhere being tended by the bandsmen who were all first aid men. The first thing I wanted was a cigarette, I wanted a fag. I was dying! I'd never smoked a lot but this time to save my nerves.... I found someone who had some fags and I just smoked my head off for a few minutes. *Private Ernie Farrow, Pioneer Section, HQ Coy, 2nd Norfolks*

All in all 26 May was a day of hard fighting in chaotic conditions. A young surviving officer attempted to piece together the shape of events assisted by notes for the Battalion War Diary kept by the Adjutant Captain Long.

During the night B and D Coys. had moved to their correct positions and were dug in by first light. B Coy. on the right of A Coy. at Petit Cornet Malo and D Coy. in the gap between C and A Coys. at 03.00 hours, the enemy made a determined attack on the B Coy. positions and a lighter attack against C Coy. on the left flank. Enemy mortar fire was extremely accurate and caused heavy casualties. Fighting in the streets of the village and several local counter-attacks by B Coy. assisted by A Coy. 1st Royal Scots failed to restore the position completely and the general situation remained obscure. In the early morning, both A and B Coys. reported that they had been very badly handled and had hardly any men left. Captains Hastings and Long were sent to reorganize both companies and to make one unit of them. This was done successfully and about 60 men continued to fight in the Petit Cornet Malo area. Lieutenant Edgeworth was reported killed and this left no officer with B Coy. Casualties were coming increasingly in all Coys. and by the early afternoon the situation was becoming desperate. Orders were received to hold the position to the last round and the last man.[3] *Lieutenant William Murray-Brown, 2nd Norfolks*

How many desperate scenes of heroism and desperation does this prosaic account conceal? We will never now know the names of any such heroes as their deeds went unrecorded except by the dead, the dying and the doomed. But, by their sacrifice, they were buying time for their retreating comrades in the main body of the BEF falling back to Dunkirk.

That afternoon the remnants of the battalion were once again re-

A Panzerkampfwagon MkII crossing the La Bassée Canal on a pontoon bridge, 27 May 1940.

IWM RML148

organised by the acting CO, Major Ryder, chiefly by means of redistributing the few surviving officers across the tattered remnants of the companies. The Germans made several inroads across the canal and although counter-attacks were vigorously launched the situation was blurred by the evening. Lance Sergeant Alden of the Bren Carrier Platoon was ordered to form a road block to the right of A Company.

At about 8.00 my gunner sighted German troops to our right and left, I warned the Corporal on my right, we fired almost all our SAA & at the same time being fired on from all directions. We got back to the farm house and reported our position.[4] *Lance Sergeant Alden, Carrier Platoon, HQ Coy, 2nd Norfolks*

On the night of 26 May an unreal calm settled and Major Ryder seized the opportunity to feed his men. Sergeant Walter Gilding had been posted from the Mortar Platoon to act as Company Quarter Master Sergeant of the Headquarters Company.

The meal was prepared, we were told where we had to go, which wasn't far anyway. I arrived at the battalion headquarters at the farm somewhere between nine and ten that evening. There was very little to be seen. Major Ryder came forward and spoke to us and said that he was glad to see us and that the food could be distributed when he could get the people off the perimeter where they were out on various defensive positions. From then on we were feeding the lads as they were coming in in dribs and drabs. We had the signallers actually in the farmhouse itself and the riflemen were out in the buildings. I can remember them being called in from their various buildings – the cowshed, the pigsties, even out in the little meadows around the farm – wherever they had taken up a position. We had special containers with lids that bolted down and it kept hot. There was no sound of shots, bombs, shellfire or anything. It went on like that all through the night till three o'clock in the morning. I was still there with the cooks' wagon still dishing out for the odd people that had been pulled in. Major Ryder came and said, "The situation seems to be getting worse". By this time it was just beginning to get daylight. "I think you'd better pack up and get back to B Echelon. But before you go report to the farmhouse where we've got the Company Headquarters and take some of the documents away because they're not much use to us here!" By the documents he meant the equipment rolls and various paperwork. It was then that I started to hear what sounded like heavy vehicles, possibly tanks moving in the distance. Also the first mortar bomb landed in the battalion area. It didn't seem to be very healthy to be there so we packed up very quickly and we were clear by half past three.

The Norfolks were up against a crack German SS unit. Here men of the Totenkopf *Division operate a mortar. The Waffen SS were easily recognizable in their camouflage smocks and helmet covers.*   Taylor Library

Coming out of the farm gate down the road to the main road in the village we were mortared down that road. There must have been six or seven mortar bombs landed along the road. I told the driver to, "Put your foot down and get the hell out of this!" Fortunately the bombs were missing us but we had quite a bumpy ride. We raced back to the B Echelon area where we found everybody was packing up ready to move. The Quartermaster had received a message from them saying that "The battalion were going to be staying in that position and that we were not to wait, that we were to go back to some other rendezvous". *Company Quartermaster Sergeant Walter Gilding, HQ Coy, 2nd Norfolks*

The storm broke at 03.30 hours on the morning of 27 May with a terrific bombardment and a crushing dawn attack on the battalion's positions. Private Arthur Brough was caught in a desperate melee as the last surviving mortar team strove to support the troops in Le Petit Cornet Malo.

We set our mortar up and it was getting a bit hectic round there. Lots of tanks and heavy gunfire. We were putting as much stuff down the mortar as we could to get rid of our ammunition. We were trying to repulse them but we knew it wasn't a lot of good because there was so many there. The Number One he was looking through the clinometer sight, focusing on roughly whereabouts the tank was situated. I was Number One. You say, "Right, on!" Tap Number Two on the shoulder. He taps Number Three who's passing the bomb over. Then they're putting it in the barrel. "Fire!" That's what we did. The mortar must have been red hot – anything they could get hold of we were putting down the mortar. There was only about three of us left by that time and Platoon Sergeant Major Ireland, he got shot. We resorted to rifle

Demolished bridges and sunken barges litter the La Bassée Canal.   IWM RML 142

fire which was absolutely stupid but I suppose it was instinct to try and do your job. Then we saw that it was absolutely hopeless we chucked the bolts out of the rifle. Why you do these things don't ask me why, but I think it must just be instinct – that's what you were taught to do – immobilize your rifle, take the bolt out. Then we scattered – tanks by the hundred were coming up – we just ran for it. What can you do when you see tanks coming at you? It was frightening really. The mortar platoon seem to have been isolated there. Johnny Cockerel, he was with me, we dived in a dyke. We got scattered dead in our tracks because there was a shell dropped quite near us from the tanks and I could feel something in the back of my leg and Johnny Cockerel he got a piece out of his knee, pretty bad. I looked after him as much as I could, just the field dressing. Mine was just a superficial cut, two or three cuts on the back of my leg and a lot of shrapnel splinters. We were in this dyke and all of a sudden the tanks were right on top of us, and the next thing we saw was a German officer standing there telling us, "The war is over, Tommy!" That's what he said. We were left there to our own devices for a little while and all their infantry was coming up behind the tanks. By that time there was a lot of them – just tanks and men. Made you wonder how you could repulse them. *Private Arthur Brough, Mortar Platoon, HQ Coy, 2nd Norfolks*

The situation was so bad that the remaining headquarters signallers were sent out to join the riflemen defending the immediate perimeter of Druries farm as German armoured formations broke through in the Le Petit Cornet Malo sector.

The tanks broke through there and they were the first ones to go out of communication. I was on the switchboard at the time and they were the first ones for us to lose. The other companies were phoning in to say that they were also being heavily attacked. Eventually the CO, Major Ryder, he ordered all surplus personnel out to the defence of battalion headquarters because we should have to make a defence on our own. So I handed over the switchboard to the wireless operator who was on the brigade radio. I went out then and the adjutant, Captain Long, told me to go forward to a row of trees, towards the front. If I saw any Germans coming between the companies and us I was to let him know. I was there for some time and no sign of anybody, so I withdrew about 100 yards or so to a farm building. There was a Regimental Police lance corporal in there and between the two of us we kept watch until he happened to look back towards battalion headquarters along the road – and there was a German motorcycle combination with a machine gun mounted on it coming from behind us. We fired and stopped the combination coming through. *Signaller R Brown, HQ Coy, 2nd Norfolks*

Men of the Totenkopf Division entering a French village during their advance towards Dunkirk in May 1940. Taylor Library

It was obvious that the Germans had broken through and that they were looking in the wrong direction.

We had to get back to battalion headquarters and let them know they were round behind us. So the two of us dashed across the road as quickly as possible, crawled along the ditch to the farm and gave the information that we had. I then took up a position in the barn. We knocked holes through the galvanized walls which were heavily riddled with shrapnel. The mortar bombs were dropping over the barn and behind us between the farm buildings. A friend of mine I was with, John Hagan said, "We'll find somewhere a bit more safe!" We went to the end of the barn and there was a small brick outhouse. We went in and knocked bricks out for loopholes. That's where we continued our defence for the remainder of the day. The other side of the farm was all the stables, cowsheds and barn stables. The men there had done the same, knocked bricks out and made loopholes so we were more or less an all round defence. We had quite a lot of wounded, at first they were in a cellar under the house, and then it was hit so many times with the shellfire and mortar bombs that it was on fire. So we had to get the wounded out and lay them in a safer place – which was a very tricky position. *Signaller R Brown, HQ Coy, 2nd Norfolks*

At some point during this last desperate phase of the action Farrow was sent out to try and blow a further bridge.

Corporal Mason shouted to me, "'Strips', come on over here!" I went across and he said, "Right, you, you and you, we've got to go and blow a bridge up. Go and find some amatol, gun cotton, whatever you can find and bring it across." He went to try and find a vehicle to take us in because we couldn't carry all this stuff around with us. Major Ryder told Corporal Mason that his driver had already been detailed to take us to this bridge, that he didn't want no map reference, he knew exactly where to go to, it was only a short distance away. The CO's vehicle was an old Humber car and the driver's name was Hawker, he came from King's Lynn. He said, "Right!" He opened the back of the old car and we put the gun cotton and primers, whatever we had we threw it in the back. The Sergeant Major came along and he said, "Right, here lads, here's something to be going with!" and he gave us a big tin of Bluebird toffees. The Quartermaster came along and he said, "It's just a few rounds!" Three rounds of ammunition we were issued with! Three rounds of ammunition to fight the German Army! We thought, "Oh, God!" With this we all piled in this old car and we were away. *Private Ernie Farrow, Pioneer Section, HQ Coy, 2nd Norfolks*

An air of desperate farce hung over this mission impossible.

We were so busy trying to get this tin lid off to get these toffees

64

Engineers of the Totenkopf *Division throw an emergency bridge across the La Bassee Canal. The Norfolks had not been able to stop them but they had made them pay dearly.* Taylor Library

out! We were being shelled and machine gunned all the way – not too badly but the occasional shot or bust of machine fire. We knew that one bullet through the back of our car and we could all be blown to pieces. We hoped to God that the driver would get there as quick as he could. In no time at all the driver turned round and said, "There you are lads, there's the bridge coming up". We all looked up – the lid was still on the toffees, we still hadn't got that off – but we looked up. This happened in seconds, not minutes. We could see the bridge in front of us and directly on our left hand side was a big house. On our right was the canal. At the very instant that he spoke a machine gun opened up and the whole top of this old car was riddled by bullets – but not one of us was touched – we were still all alive, not even a scratch. We didn't wait for the second burst, we dived out, because the Germans were firing from this house. So there was no point in us trying to get to the bridge because they were already over it. We were straight into the canal. The driver he was trying to turn his vehicle round, to get back to headquarters to warn them that this bridge had already been taken – I suppose that's what was in his mind. By the time we got into the canal we heard this hell of an explosion and we were spattered by all the pieces of metal and whatnot as the poor old car was blown up and the driver with it. We tried to climb up to the edge of the canal bank and fire at the Germans. Somehow we managed to get a footing, how we did I don't know, because a canal is all mud on the bank. It was a heck of a job but we managed to get there and we fired our few rounds off at these Germans in the house and along the side of the bridge, hoping that every bullet would kill a German. *Private Ernie Farrow, Pioneer Section, HQ Coy, 2nd Norfolks*

With only three rounds apiece they had soon fired their last shot and it was apparent that they were going to have real difficulties in getting back to battalion headquarters.

There was no way we could get out of the canal where we were. So Corporal Mason told us, "Right, bolts out of your rifles, get rid of them, because there's no way they're needed any more". Our tin hats, everything went off into the canal. The Germans were on both sides so it made no difference where we went but we felt it safer to go on over the other side because we couldn't get out of the canal. The banks were too high to climb and if you started to climb the banks you'd be picked off. Luckily for us we were all good swimmers and we swam underwater most of the way across because as soon as you came up you were fired at. We came up on the other side under this bed of rushes. We just kept still to stop even the ripples in the water for fear that the Germans would put machine guns into where we were. The Corporal said, "Right, stop where you are, keep your heads down. I'm going to swim down the canal and find somewhere where there's a ditch runs into the canal where we can climb out. That's the only safe way we can get out, we can't get out where we are now". Then he disappeared. *Private Ernie Farrow, Pioneer Section, HQ Coy, 2nd Norfolks*

Farrow and his companions were left in an extremely exposed position, unarmed, up to their necks in deep water – both literally and figuratively.

The three of us were very close together in these rushes, they were about two foot either side of me – I was in the centre. This young fellow on my left hand side, almost touching me, his name was Porter and he came from Beccles in Suffolk. He'd been in the army with me from the time we joined up, a very nice young fellow and he said to me, "I'm just going to have a peek over the top". At that very instant I heard this machine gun or rifle fire and I thought that they'd fired across into the bank of this canal and I turned and looked up. This poor fellow had been shot right through the middle of his head and the back of his head was missing. As quick as that and he was sinking back in the water. I was trying to hold him up which was no good, because he was already dead. This fellow on my right, his name was Reeve he came from Dickleborough in Suffolk. Now he was an old soldier and he'd been out in India and had two gold teeth put in the top of his plate. I was talking to him, telling him about poor old Porter, and I felt something hit my face. I put my hand up automatically and I was covered in blood. I thought, "God!" I looked at the blood and thought I'd been hit. I felt again but I was still all there. When I turned round to look it was this poor fellow. What had happened was they'd shot his jaw and his jaw had smacked me in the face. He was then disappearing underneath – the last thing I saw of him was these two gold teeth shining in the top of his head and for many, many weeks afterwards, whenever I opened my eyes, I could see his face with no chin and his gold teeth showing. The water round me was red with the blood but the poor boys they'd gone – they were at the bottom. *Private Ernie Farrow, Pioneer Section, HQ Coy, 2nd Norfolks*

The severely traumatized Farrow was thus left on his own.

A few minutes afterwards the Corporal came back, I didn't see him, I didn't see a ripple in the water. All I knew was he came up at the side of me and he knew exactly what had happened. He said, "Right, we can't fret about the poor boys, let's go". We dived under and we swam. How far we swam I've got no idea, we came up for a drop of air here and there. Eventually he pulled on me and said, "Here we are", and there was this ditch right beside us. The first thing I wanted to do was get out of that damn canal, to get clear of it, I'd seen enough damage already. He said, "You stop where you are – that's an order – keep your head down. I'll go have a look see if there's anything on this meadow." As I was standing in this canal I looked down this ditch and on the left hand side I could see a bush, and I was almost sure I could see this bush moving. I heard this mouthful of army language come out, I looked and 'Misler' had been shot through the shoulder and the bone of his arm was sticking out the top. He put his arm around my neck to keep himself up and again everything happened in seconds. This bush I'd seen, there was a German behind it, probably the one who'd shot 'Mis'. Just then, he came from behind this bush, jumped in this ditch and he came running down towards us. When he was about 12 yards from us he stopped and put his rifle up to his shoulder. I said my last prayer because I knew I was going to die. But the Lord was with me and there was a loud click – he'd run out of ammunition or his breech had stuck – there was no bullet came out, no bang. He jumped down towards us and he knew he'd got us exactly where he wanted us, we couldn't move. He turned his rifle round, got hold of the barrel and as he got close to us he took a swipe at my head. I put my arm up to stop him hitting me and the first blow smashed all my hand up. The next blow came down and I still had the strength to hold my elbow up to stop him and he smashed my elbow and put my shoulder out of joint. One more blow and I'd have been dead but at that very instant I heard this loud shout and lots more Germans came into sight. One of these was an officer who'd shouted. They jumped into this ditch and he ordered them to pull us out of the canal. They pulled out poor 'Mis' first. They'd got to be very careful because if they pulled his wrong arm they'd have pulled it off he was in such a state. But he was still alive and they put him on a stretcher and took him away. They pulled me out. *Private Ernie Farrow, Pioneer Section, HQ Coy, 2nd Norfolks*

Farrow was indeed lucky to survive the war. After a short spell as a POW, he escaped and managed to make his way, via Switzerland, back home to Norwich.

Back at Druries Farm the situation was becoming desperate as one by one the perimeter defence companies were over-run. The Germans were well and truly across the canal in strength, it was increasingly obvious that the Headquarters Company was cut off and that the situation was hopeless.

Towards the afternoon Major Ryder came round to us and said there was no way we could get away from where we were, ammunition was running very low and he was taking opinions as to how we felt about fighting on or surrendering. "Well", some said, "Fight on!" Some said, "Surrender!" I said, "Well, let's carry

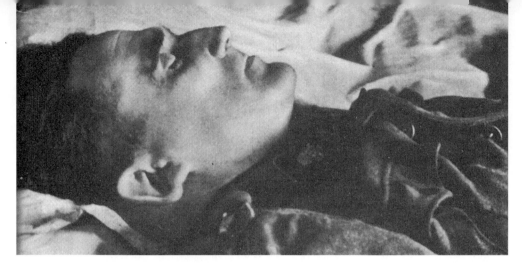

The Norfolks had put up a hard fight against elements of the SS Totenkopf Division – the Nazis' stormtroopers had lost their Regimental Commander, Standartenfuehrer Hans Friedmann Goetze (above seen here laid out in a French farmhouse near Le Paradis). Below: Men of the Totenkopf during the campaign. Did men of this SS division take vengeance out on the Norfolks for the death of their commander? Taylor Library

British prisoners being led away from the La Bassée battlefield, 27 May 1940. They were fortunate in having been captured by elements of the Wehrmacht rather than one of the Waffen SS units. The Norfolks were up against the Totenkopf *and for them it was to be a different outcome.*   IWM RML 141

on as we are!" Because the morale was very high – there was no thought of being taken prisoner, getting killed or wounded. We were just carrying on fighting, carrying on the defence and making a joke of it all really. Laughing and joking between each other. We were causing more casualties than they were causing to us but at that time I should think they must have outnumbered us by about six to one. Eventually he said that it was no good wasting human life, we couldn't hold them up indefinitely, we'd held them up for three days on the canal which was a very good effort and he'd decided that we should have to cease firing. But he said if anybody thought they could get away, then we were entitled to do our own thing – we wouldn't be running away from the battalion, we would be trying to get away and save ourselves. The men in the outbuildings and the stables went through the stable door to the field. At first they were fired on so they came back in and then after a time they went out again with a dirty white towel on a rifle to wave and they were allowed to go out. *Signaller R Brown, HQ Coy, 2nd Norfolks*

The fate of this party of men who left through the stable door owed nothing to conventional warfare. Their surrender had been accepted and the 'dangerous' part seemed to be over as they and a few other troops captured nearby were marched away from Druries Farm by the No 3 Company of the 1st Battalion, 2nd SS Totenkopf Regiment under the command of Fritz Knoechlein.

> There were a hundred of us prisoners marching in column of threes. We turned off the dusty French road through a gateway and into a meadow beside the buildings of a farm. I saw, with one of the nastiest feelings I've ever had in my life, two heavy machine-guns inside the meadow. They were manned and pointing at the head of our column. I felt as though an icy hand gripped my stomach. The guns began to spit fire and even as the front men began to fall I said fiercely, "This can't be. They can't do this to us!" For a few seconds the cries and shrieks of our stricken men drowned the cracking of the guns. Men fell like grass before a scythe. The invisible blade came nearer and then swept through me. I felt a terrific searing pain in my left leg and wrist and pitched forward in a red world of tearing agony. My scream of pain mingled with the cries of my mates but even as I fell forward into a heap of dying men the thought stabbed my brain, "If I ever get out of here the swine who did this will pay for it". *Signaller Albert Pooley, A Coy, 2nd Norfolks*[5]

In those terrible moments 97 men were cut down. As the German SS troops moved amongst the sprawling bodies they administered the coup de grace by bullet and bayonet to all those who looked like they might still be breathing. In this horrific situation Pooley received another two bullets in his left leg but, by a supreme act of will, he kept still and thus survived until the SS butchers had left the scene of the crime. Only one other man had survived the massacre, Signaller William O'Callaghan, who had been lucky enough to escape with just an arm wound beneath the shattered corpses of his friends. O'Callaghan helped drag the crippled Pooley from that awful pile of bodies. Although both were recaptured a few days later, they survived the war to wreak their vengeance on Knoechlein, when they had the satisfaction of acting as prosecution witnesses at a British Military Court in Hamburg in October 1948. As a result Knoechlein was found guilty and hanged on 29 January 1949. Pooley had kept his promise.

Brown and his little group had made the right decision not to accompany Major Ryder by sheer luck.

The barn wall in front of which the prisoners were machine-gunned down. Evidence of the massacre at Louis Creton's farm can be seen in the chest-high line of bullet hole scars on the wall.

Myself, John Hagan and another pal of mine, Bill Leven, decided we would go out of the door on to the road which was in the opposite direction to the others. The smoke from the burning house was going that way so we thought we'd keep in the smoke as extra cover in the hopes of getting away. We went in a ditch at the side of the road and in the ditch was the adjutant, lying on the ground wounded and the medical officer was there. We attempted to go out of the ditch and cross the road but as we did so the German patrols were coming up from the village of Le Paradis and we just couldn't get over the road. They just shouted, "Hands up!" or words to that effect and that was that. They pushed and knocked us about a bit but nothing outrageous. *Signaller R Brown, HQ Coy, 2nd Norfolks*

The fighting strength of the battalion had almost all been killed, wounded, captured or massacred. Only the drivers and cooks of the B Echelon were left to try and escape. Their problems were by no means over.

The refugee problem was really terrible then and it was difficult to get transport along the roads. It was basically just the cook element who had the cooks' trucks and the quartermaster with his stores truck that were trying to get back to wherever – we didn't even know about Dunkirk then. All we were informed was that we were going back to another rendezvous. It was absolute chaos. Five miles would take half a day. If the Stukas came down we would dive off the lorries and get into the hedgerows or ditches and the refugees would do the same. They wouldn't be so quick on the

British soldiers killed in the fighting as they covered the withdrawal to Dunkirk. An SS officer checks for signs of life. Taylor Library

mark as us so we would pile back into the lorry and drive through before the refugees assembled onto the roadways again. But you wouldn't go far before you came unstuck again and they'd all be on the road again with their handcarts, baggage, horse and carts – you name it – everything was there. By this time we had got split up. With the refugee problem it was difficult to keep two or three vehicles together. *Company Quartermaster Sergeant Walter Gilding, HQ Coy, 2nd Norfolks*

They were getting nowhere fast and Gilding had to face up to reality.

We were on the road with the truck for two days and things got so bad that we just had to abandon the vehicle. It was just impossible, I suppose in two days we had moved 15-20 miles at the most. I had to make a decision whether to sit in the lorry and see whether the situation would get better and it was obviously getting worse all the time, or dispose of the truck and hitchhike, walk, march, whatever... This is what we decided to do. There was a small sort of canal by the road and there were vehicles already in

The fleeing refugees hindered the movement of British troops. Taylor Library

there so took the opportunity of doing the same. The driver drained the sump and ran the engine till it seized up then we just pushed it in the canal. *Company Quartermaster Sergeant Walter Gilding, HQ Coy, 2nd Norfolks*

Gilding's stripes attracted a few other stragglers and on foot they made their way to Dunkirk from which they had heard the evacuation was taking place.

Fleeing to the c

It was chaotic, buildings were smoking, smouldering, there was ruins. The church was standing there, all the front of it pitted with bomb splinters and bullets. As I passed the church there was two Scotsman from the Royal Scots stood with a civilian against the door with fixed bayonets. I didn't intervene but as I went past I thought, "I know what it is, we've been told about fifth columnist and they've probably got someone under suspicion there. We arrived at one end of the beach where all the sand dunes were. There was a beachmaster, a naval officer, directing the lads on the beaches. He said, "New arrivals, Sergeant, just take the far end of the sand dunes and dig in facing the other way." We had ten rifles and I think everyone had some ammunition. We went to the allocated place and dug in. We stayed there that night which would be the 30th/31st. We had a bird's eye view from where we were. Watching all the lads lining up down to the water's edge ready to be evacuated with gaps of 20-30 yards between each group – there must have been ten of these queues. Out in the water, way out on the horizon, were naval destroyers and also civilian boats – private yachts and all types of boats. Plying in between the beach and them were small boats – some just rowing boats. I thought, "God, they're going take a long while to get this lot off!" An oil depot had been bombed, it was burning and the smoke was blowing across the beach which was a Godsend really because it was more or less a camouflage and the Germans couldn't see the beaches themselves. I thought, "Well there's no way we're going to hold up the whole German Army! It's just a matter of time – we shall be either over-run, captured or hopefully we're going to be evacuated!" *Company Quartermaster Sergeant Walter Gilding, HQ Coy, 2nd Norfolks*

Sands of Dunk

In fact, through the desperate efforts of the Royal Navy and the civilian volunteers in their 'little ships' who swarmed across the English Channel, they were offered sanctuary in the early hours of the morning of 1 June.

Safely in Engl

They said, "Take your group down to the edge of the water and whatever boat comes in you will be next on the list!" By this time there were very few on the beach. One boat came in that couldn't get in because it was too shallow. The second or third boat that came in must have been flat bottomed and we all piled on to it but

found that it wouldn't take off because it was stuck on the sands. Several of us had to get out and push it until we could float. Then we were taken out to a larger vessel which was a Belgian pleasure boat. I was pulled over the side, shown down into the cabin, it held four people and there was about 20 of us in there. Some of them just had to stand, there was no room to even sit down. We were given some blankets and a hot drink. For myself and several of the others we just dropped off to sleep jammed in that cabin. I was told but I didn't know anything about it that we were machine gunned on the way out. I hadn't had any sleep, except catnaps, you sort of shut your eyes wandering along half asleep, since we left Le Paradis. I woke when we arrived at Dover, somebody said, "Come on lads, we're here, you're in England!" *Company Quartermaster Sergeant Walter Gilding, HQ Coy, 2nd Norfolks*

The relief was incredible but many men felt a sense of guilt at having survived and, strangely, given the circumstances, a nagging feeling that perhaps they had let their country down.

When we went ashore I thought everybody was going to shoot us, especially being a regular soldier, we'd run away – that was the feeling I had. But instead of that there were people cheering and clapping us as if we were heroes. Giving us mugs of tea and sandwiches. We looked a sorry sight I think – like scruffy soldiers. *Company Quartermaster Sergeant Walter Gilding, HQ Coy, 2nd Norfolks*

For the wounded there were still tragedies in miniature to endure. Private Ernie Leggett had been evacuated to the Royal County Hospital at Brighton. Here he met an old friend.

Walter Gilding

The sister of the ward came to me and she said, "There's somebody in the next ward who has ordered that he should see you!" I said, "Well who is it?" She said, "Wait and see when you get in there!" They had to lift me out, put me on a wheel chair, they wheeled me in and I was greeted with, "Hello, Boy, how are you?" It was Sergeant Major Gristock! I saw the cage over his legs and he told me his legs had been so shot up by the broadside of this machine gun that they had to amputate his legs from the hip. I noticed that on his bed rail was a line of about 10 or 12 bottles of ale and it immediately went through my mind that a man in such a condition as he was in – if they allowed him to drink then he must be in a very poor way. He said, "Do something for me, Boy?" I said, "Yes, what's that?" He said, "Fill this up for me!" He couldn't do it himself, he had to be fed and everything. He'd got one of these things like a little teapot with a handle on the end. I filled it with beer and held it to his mouth and he just supped this bottle of ale. He said, "Cor, pour another one in!" I did that and I did that every day I went through to see him. I told him, "I saw what you did". He said, "Yes, the bastards, but I wiped them out, I got the so and sos!" To me he seemed as if he was getting better. We talked in army parlance about the old days, how we'd played football matches and sport... I used to stay with him for half an hour or an hour. Every day they'd wheel me through. Then that horrible morning came on the 16th June when they hadn't come and got me. I said to the nurse, "Nurse, take me through to see my Sergeant Major!" She said, "No, sorry..." *Private Ernie Leggett, A Coy, 2nd Norfolks*

Gristock, who was posthumously awarded the VC he so richly deserved for his actions on the Escaut Canal, and most of the rest of Leggett's pals from the original battalion were dead. But the 2nd Norfolks would be back at the sharp end before the war was over.

Hauptsturmfuehrer Fritz Knoechlein
Commander of No.3 Company, the Totenkopf 2nd Infantry Regiment.
He was awarded the Ritterkreuz *in 1944 and finished the war with the rank of Obersturmbannfuehrer.*

Knoechlein was held responsible for the murder of 97 men of the 2nd Royal Norfolk Regiment. There were two survivors of the massacre, Private Albert Pooley and Private William O'Callaghan, they were among the witnesses that helped bring him to justice. He was tried in October 1948 and hanged at Hamburg on 28th January 1949.

CHAPTER FIVE

Rebuilding

The battered remnants of the Norfolks were concentrated at Idle on the outskirts of Bradford in Yorkshire in early June 1940. A huge draft of some 350 men was sent from the Infantry Training Centres of the Essex and Royal Berkshire Regiments at Blandford Camp in Dorset. This draft was formed from wartime conscripts who were just completing their six months' basic training. Most were not overly concerned at losing their original cap badges.

> We were all Berkshires then, but suddenly we were told that we were transferred – we would now be in the Royal Norfolk Regiment. We would keep our numbers and be issued with new cap badges, which was the Britannia. One or two blokes were, "Ooooh, I don't go a lot on this, what's it all about?" You know, but it didn't make any difference – our pay wasn't altered – it was no big deal! It was just a different regiment, we didn't know – we hadn't got a clue who they were until we got to Bradford. *Lance Corporal Ben Macrae, A Coy, 2nd Norfolks*

There was the usual regionalistic banter to enliven the atmosphere.

Fred Rolleston

> There was a little bit of rivalry, in so much of course that they were Norfolks and the majority of us posted were Londoners – Cockneys! One of the early mornings the lance corporal, a Norfolk, came round to call us. His brogue was, "Come you on, you over here and get on up, out of it!" From underneath the blankets the whole chorus came out, "SWEDE!" He wasn't very pleased! *Private Fred Rolleston, D Coy, 2nd Norfolks*

Some of the new drafts, aware that they were meant to be joining a regular battalion, were a little disturbed at the un-military appearance of the Dunkirk veterans.

> We'd been highly trained and when we saw these dishevelled soldiers we were a bit upset. We were a little bit surprised that this was the regular army just turned up and not looking in very good shape. But that was very unfair of us. *Private Dennis Boast, Carrier Platoon, HQ Coy, 2nd Norfolks*

The reasons were however perfectly obvious when the mail finally caught up with them.

> There were several of them standing round and the post sergeant was sorting out sacks of mail. As he was pulling out letters from the mail bags they were saying such things as, "No, he copped it! No, he copped it! He's back!" Right through these

sacks of mail. It sounded very bad. *Corporal Bill Seymour, 2nd Norfolks*

George Winter

The battalion moved to a new camp at Driffield Woods on 22 July and the same day their new commanding officer arrived. Lieutenant-Colonel George Winter was a slightly enigmatic figure

> Very eccentric. If we went out on a scheme somewhere, or a route march he would lay in wait for you. He knew the route you were coming and he'd hide himself somewhere. We'd be marching along and then you'd hear a voice shout out, "What is that man doing with his rifle!" You didn't know where he was, we were all looking round – we didn't know where the voice was coming from! We thought someone was pulling our leg! *Private Stan Roffey, Carrier Platoon, HQ Coy, 2nd Norfolks*

The battalion received a draft of a number of regular NCOs from the 1st Battalion, Royal Norfolk Regiment who had recently returned from India. Their role was to help stiffen the drafts of new recruits flooding in from the depot at Britannia Barracks and from other regiments. Amongst these 'old sweats' was the imposing figure of Corporal Bert Fitt already a veteran of seven years' service. He was not initially impressed by what he found.

> They were already a cadre for NCOs in the company, and the instructor was a Corporal Sculthorpe. Now he was self-taught and I had to go on this cadre from the day I arrived there. Of course nobody knew anything about me and the first day the chap was teaching wrong. He was just teaching the positions as he saw them, or as he thought of them. No laid down sequence at all. This is what upset me. After the day had finished I got the instructor and told him that he was teaching wrong. He complained to the Company Sergeant Major who sent for me, gave me a rocket, and put me before the Company Commander over it. When I went before the Company Commander I told him what certificates I held, and he asked the Sergeant Major, "Is this correct? Well, why is he on a cadre under Sculthorpe, when he should be taking it?" I was immediately put in charge of the cadre. *Corporal Bert Fitt, A Coy, 2nd Norfolks*

Corporal Fitt was rapidly promoted to Sergeant and his hard won experience was put to good use in the months of training that followed. Amongst the drafts flooding in from other regiments to rebuild the shattered battalion was a large draft from the Royal Warwickshire Regiment. These men swiftly earned themselves an unenviable reputation.

> Well, like every other battalion, if you transfer men from one battalion to the other, you obviously don't transfer your best men. So we got a mixed bag. Quite a number of them had been called

up for service and didn't care what they did, or what happened to them. They weren't very helpful. Some of them were quite terrors, they'd go out and cause trouble if they could, chiefly fighting. Going out, getting drunk, missing the bus home and being late coming in. *Sergeant Bert Fitt, A Coy, 2nd Norfolks*

Officers also came from various sources. One, Sam Hornor, a member of a prosperous family of land agents based in Norwich whose father had served with distinction with the 2nd Battalion, Norfolk Regiment in Mesopotamia, knew exactly what path he wanted to follow. Advised by his father on the outset of war to be patient before enlisting, he first took the opportunity to taste life as a student at Trinity College Cambridge and found it perfectly acceptable.

I joined the boat club and that was fun, they did it just like the old days – all the boat club sat at a separate table in hall and it was rather like being in a piggery! You were fed with steak and red wine, chocolate or treacle pudding and port! To get you all strong for applying it to your oar! All very amusing but there it was. The general attitude that year, '39-'40 in Cambridge was, "Eat, drink and be merry, for tomorrow we die!" *Sam Hornor*

From there he went to and Officers' Cadet Training Unit before receiving his commission in 1940. At this point the 'old boys' network swung into smooth action.

We then had to fill in a form about posting – what regiment. I just wrote down, "The Royal Norfolk Regiment" and put my line through the two alternatives. He said, "You must put down more than one – you may not get there!" I said, "Well, Sir, it's all arranged because you see my father's very friendly with the Colonel of the Regiment and they've arranged that I am to be commissioned in to the Royal Norfolk Regiment and posted to the 2nd Battalion – my father's old Battalion!" "Oh well", he said, "You've learnt a lot about the army already!" And that is duly of course what happened. *Officer Cadet Sam Hornor*

When these young inexperienced officers finally arrived at the battalion they passed under the jaundiced eye of their NCOs who had forgotten more than the ingenues would ever know. Hornor found himself in command of the newly promoted Sergeant Fitt.

I was received and welcomed, they knew I was coming, they knew a bit about my history and they knew my father was a famous First World War member. I found myself posted to 8 Platoon in A Company which was my father's old company and platoon. I was introduced to my Platoon Sergeant – one Sergeant Fitt! I thought when I first saw him, "My Godfathers, he's going to be a difficult one!" He was a pretty tough looking old soldier to me – although he obviously wasn't very old. In practice he was very helpful because I had the sense to ask him when I was stuck as to what to do next! When doing some training I might say to him, "I don't know, how the hell are we going to deal with this one?" And he'd say, "This is what I'd do, Sir!" It really worked quite well and we got to know each other quite well. *Second Lieutenant Sam Hornor, A Coy, 2nd Norfolks*

One story perhaps perfectly exemplifies the situation.

> We used to go out on these firing ranges and this young second lieutenant gave the order, "One round, rapid fire!" We nicknamed him 'One round rapid' from that day onwards! *Corporal Bill Seymour, 2nd Norfolks*

There was another officer posted to the battalion who could not in any way be described as young, inexperienced or diffident. Major Robert Scott was a former regular officer who had served in the First World War. He had a unique way of drawing attention to himself that was quite simply unforgettable, armed, as he often was, with a sawn off .303 Lee Enfield.

> The day after I arrived A Company were on the range and I was told to go on the range with them. I didn't know what on earth I was supposed to do and I stood there wondering when suddenly there was the most awful explosion down my right ear and a sheet of flame. I thought, "God! What's happened?" It was followed by, "Ha, ha, ha – I'm Scott! I heard you were coming!" That was my welcome by Robert Scott! He then said, "Have you heard of 'Little Willie' here?" I said, "Yes I have, Sir! My father's told me all about him!" "Well", he said, "you're going to fire it down the range, I'll show you how to do it – you take it out and you have that arm absolutely rigid! If it's bent you'll kill yourself – so have it rigid!" So it was loaded and I held it absolutely rigid, fired and actually hit the target – but my arm went back, straight over my head! Terrifying weapon! It was typical Robert! He was really a most dreadful fellow when he wasn't being shot at! *Second Lieutenant Sam Hornor, A Coy, 2nd Norfolks*

Hornor's father did indeed have cause to remember his contacts with Scott with whom he had served at Felixstowe Camp in the First World War.

> There was a young subaltern there who really was a scourge to everybody called Second Lieutenant Scott. My father got quite friendly with Robert Scott who was mad then! One night when a lot of them were coming back from the pub there was chaos in the camp, everybody was flat on the deck because Robert Scott was firing from his tent in all directions. The only way they could stop him was to crawl forward and pull out the tent pegs, fell his tent on top of him and then beat him senseless with tent pegs. But

according to my father he was quite all right the next morning. *Second Lieutenant Sam Hornor, A Coy, 2nd Norfolks*

Another young second lieutenant whose father had commanded Scott later in the war found that he was taken under his wing.

Robert Scott

He said, "Are you by any chance the son of 'Borneo' Davies?" I said, "Yes, my father was in Borneo!" He said, "I was his subaltern, I'll teach you to be a bloody good soldier like he was! I'll teach you all your father would have taught you". I think he chased me unduly hard to make sure I did things right – he said, "I owe this to your father!" *Second Lieutenant Dickie Davies, D Coy, 2nd Norfolks*

Whatever their rank, gradually every man in the Norfolks came to know Scott by sight and sound.

I was making my way down to D Company for the first time and I passed through B Company lines. Major Scott was outside his tent shaving and I walked past him and he bellowed out, "Come back, that man!" I went across to him and he said, "Don't you normally salute officers?" Considering the fact he was stripped to the waist I didn't even know who he was, so I said, "I'm sorry, Sir, but I didn't notice you!" "The biggest bloody man in the British Army and you didn't notice me!!" *Private Fred Hazell, D Coy, 2nd Norfolks*

Physically he was an imposing figure, loud, abrasive, but somehow strangely reassuring for men who knew that they would have to fight face to face with enemy infantry.

He was a big bloke, over six foot and he was broad as well. They made a song up about him, "Ten thousand miles away one can hear him...." He was born after his time – he should have been born in the Elizabethan era – he could have sunk the old Armada on his own. *Bugler Bert May, HQ Coy, 2nd Norfolks*

Gradually all these disparate elements were forged together to form the 'new' 2nd Battalion, Royal Norfolk Regiment. Now a regular battalion only in name, it was nevertheless being moulded into a formidable fighting force which would have been a credit to the pre–war army.

Good steady old Norfolk chaps, many of them regular soldiers, a lot of drafts from the Royal Warwicks – Brums, and the best of the Brums were absolutely first class. Then a lot of cockneys from various London sources – and they were marvellous. We were putting all this together as a coherent battalion, weeding out the bad ones, as you do, posting them back to the depot – with a bad foot or something – any old excuse. Quite ruthlessly get rid of bad ones and keep good ones until we were all working very well together and it was a marvellous combination – especially when bullets were flying about. The steady old Norfolk chap, very steady, plodding on; the mercurial cockney, wanting to go faster, rushing about like a mad thing – the two of those gelled together to form a marvellous combination. *Second Lieutenant Sam Hornor, A Coy, 2nd Norfolks*

There was still a long way to go before they could prove themselves in action and in the meantime there was a mountain of training to climb. Weapons training, route marches, tactical exercises, rapid deployment schemes; all against a background of endless specialist training in mortars, Bren carriers, Bren guns, signals and all the myriad cornucopia of equipment needed by a modern infantry battalion at war. They were not to know that Hitler would not invade that summer of 1940 and there was a real urgency about the anti-parachutist exercises. Meanwhile the Lufftwaffe sent a reminder that they had by no means gone away.

We were on a route march, almost back to camp, when Driffield airport was bombed in great strength. A whole load of bombers came over and they plastered the place. On the radio that evening, 'Lord Haw Haw' said, "We saw you Norfolks all scurrying for cover! It's your turn next!" Everybody just sort of poked their fingers up at the thought of it. The most dramatic thing was they left one hangar standing. The following day they sent one bomber over on it's own and it flattened the last hangar. Quite incredible! *Private Fred Hazell, D Coy, 2nd Norfolks*

In the post-Dunkirk paranoia about fifth column activities and general spy scares it was considered essential to set up anti-espionage patrols.

There was a lot of reports of enemy spies – lights shining from the trees in the woods. We used to have a patrol go round, an NCO with five or six chaps with you. You'd go all around the grounds looking out for any lights or any suspicious things. It was very eerie at times walking through these woods and the fields – you'd hear a rustle and when you got closer there was a big fat cow standing there! *Corporal Bill Seymour, 2nd Norfolks*

Amidst the general chaos the usual give and take of army life flourished.

George Lee he was a bit of a comedian, always getting up to tricks. George said to me, "Stan, we'll have a laugh here! Come with me we'll go into the signals tent" We went into the tent and they were all sitting there and George said, "Guess what's happened? There's louse in the camp and we've all got to have our hair cut off from our privates and under the armpits!" "Oh Christ!" We left their tent and went back, then George said to me,

Stan Roffey

"Let's have a look and see what they're doing!" When we went in they'd got their trousers down and there they were cutting their hair off their privates with the scissors from their 'housewife'. *Private Stan Roffey, Carrier Platoon, HQ Coy, 2nd Norfolks*

An even more successful joke was played on the Provost Sergeant.

The Provost Sergeant's name was Cassidy, nicknamed 'Hopalong' naturally. He, like several of the older soldiers, liked his glass of ale and he often came home a bit tiddly at night. In these woods it used to be pitch dark and it was muddy, there was all these bell tents with all the ropes all over the place. The Regimental Police part of the woods was right up in an isolated corner. So he could find his way through easily to his own tent, he'd lined the passage way with luminous bark which was prevalent in these woods from a certain species of tree. He came in at night and just walked down in between these lines of luminous bark into his own tent. One night some of us thought we'd play a joke on old 'Hopalong' so we re-directed this luminous bark so that it led right into a slit trench! Lo and behold, 'Hopalong' came home – 'Whoosh' – straight in the trench! Some years afterwards he joined the London branch. One night we told him about this, "Oh it was you bastards he said! I got scratched to blazes!" But at least he could see the funny side of it! *Corporal Bill Seymour, 2nd Norfolks*

One horror, not in any way related to Nazi Germany, was inflicted on the battalion by some of the well meaning citizens of Driffield and the surrounding area.

Some of these concert parties laid on by church societies and things like that consisted of dear little old ladies who would stand up and sing 'Rule Britannia'. Pretty awful stuff really. So of course the lads just used to disappear and after ten minutes there was nobody in the marquee. The Company Commander said, "Hazell, you'll patrol the outside of the marquee and don't let anybody leave!" So if I saw anybody climbing underneath the side walls I stamped on their fingers and they went back in again! *Private Fred Hazell, 2nd Bn, D Coy, RNR*

As the colder weather set in the living conditions in the tents steadily deteriorated until in October the battalion was moved to the village of Hessle which lay opposite Hull across the Humber. They were billeted in large requisitioned houses. The officers naturally established a proper mess and so the new officers with only six months' service began to get to know the few who had survived the murderous campaign in France.

They were a bit cliquey. There were some officers that I almost didn't come to know. There were only 30 of us or so in the mess, those in my own company I naturally soon came to know because

Maurice Franses

we were working together all day long. But otherwise little cliques used to develop. It was quite competitive between the officers, one felt it, competing for the favour of the senior officers. There were quite a lot of regular officers still there, and there was a bit of a gap. Some overcame it better than others. Murray-Brown was very good at that – he was a regular but it didn't make any difference. I can understand the regulars taking that view a little bit, after all they joined the army before the war and they had their rules, then all of a sudden they were being invaded by all these outsiders. *Second Lieutenant Maurice Franses, 2nd Norfolks*

The young officers were constantly under informal observation by their seniors who, not unnaturally, sought to determine who would and would not make the grade. One important indication of character was drinking habits.

I personally drank very little. But of course one had one's mess bill which was very, very carefully kept, very discreetly done. I soon became aware that the size of one's mess bill was of great interest to the C.O. because it was an indication of behaviour – or could be – because 90% of what was on the mess bill was drink. *Second Lieutenant Maurice Franses, 2nd Norfolks*

Meanwhile the Regimental Sergeant Major Gordon Wright was keen on establishing a properly functioning Sergeants' mess where they were a little less fussy about drinking.

If you got a good sergeants' mess, you got a good battalion. You can always guarantee that. They worked together, always ready to listen to anything that came up. Always keen to help one another. You eat in the mess with your own cooks and your own menu. If you got a good sergeants' mess you always had somebody who could boost up your rations from the outside world. You had your bar – I used to drink about ten or twelve pints of beer in a session. No, it never affected me the next morning. Mind you if you went over the top at night, and you had any doubts about yourself, you'd take an aspro before you go to bed with your last drink. You'd wake up the next morning and you wouldn't know you'd had a drink. You could drink what you liked providing you could

Gordon Wright

stand on your feet and you were sensible. Nobody would say anything to you. But if you got drunk so you fell down, that was a disgrace and you'd be in hot water the next day. You would form your own entertainment in the mess, amongst the members. If it was possible to have any guests come into the mess you'd have them in and make them welcome. You had your dartboards, you had your cards. But after about half past eight at night you'd most probably have somebody singing, you made your own entertainment by members of the mess doing different things themselves. The RSM was very, very good on poetry and one of his pet pieces of poetry was a piece called, 'Spotty was my chum he was – a ginger headed lad'. That was something that used to go down well. *Sergeant Bert Fitt, A Coy, 2nd Norfolks*

To a newly promoted hostilities-only sergeant the atmosphere of such an old style regular sergeants' mess could be a little intimidating. One young sergeant who did not drink found a friendly, but insistent, pressure to conform

> When I was promoted to Sergeant I walked into the Sergeants' Mess and the Regimental Sergeant Major said, "What are you having, Sergeant?" I said, "I don't drink!" He said, "Nonsense, everybody drinks in the Sergeants' Mess!" So I had a shandy! When it came to my turn to pay, I said, "I'll have a shandy!" He turned round to the Mess Sergeant and said, "Charge him the same price as beer, Sergeant!" So after that I drank beer! *Sergeant Fred Rolleston, D Coy, 2nd Norfolks*

The tales of far off places and long gone characters could unintentionally be exclusive, creating a wall between the regulars and the conscripts.

> I was probably the second conscript to enter the sergeants' mess. For a long, long time it was very difficult to join in the conversation because they were all talking about what they did in Egypt in 1931 and what happened in Poona in 1933. Do you remember old 'so and so' and this, that and the other. You were completely left out. You just sort of sat there and listened. Slowly of course more conscripts came into the mess and in the end there was quite a good blend. *Sergeant Fred Hazell, D Coy, 2nd Norfolks*

The men roamed the cheery taverns of Hessle. They could drink what they liked without comment from their peer group but were restricted by lack of money. In the main they made their own entertainment.

> At the other end of the water's edge, about half a mile towards the mouth of the Humber, was a pub that we'd found called the Ferryboat Inn. Ark Hill and I went in for a drink and there was nobody about at all. We said to the governor, "Would you like a bit of music of an evening?" He said, "Bwwhrr, music - I'd like

someone to come and listen to it!" So we said, "We'll bring a small band down!" We did and a few people did come and the Governor said, "When can you come again?" "We'll come tomorrow night!" There was a piano accordion player, Pedlar Palmer, who was brilliant. He couldn't read a note of music but he could play anything you ever wanted to hear! Ark Hill was on the violin, Stan Billiard who was the funniest man you ever met, played the violin as well – sort of! He was a joker, he used to lead it – the master of ceremonies. He sang everything. The drummer used to play professionally at a dance hall in Norwich. We played dance music and sing song. In the end the bus service had been extended from Hull to go to the Ferryboat Inn to unload all the people who wanted to go. The governor used to start the kitty off with five shillings and our sergeant used to go round with his cap and collect a few pennies – but we didn't do it for the money really – although it came in handy! *Private Dennis Boast, Carrier Platoon, Headquarters Coy, 2nd Norfolks*

The landlord was sympathetic to soldiers and did all he could to keep them entertained whilst of course bolstering his profits which must have suffered terribly when the local lads were called up.

The Governor used to organize these darts matches, inter company matches. Anyone that got a 'ton' he used to give a free pint to! *Corporal Bill Seymour, 2nd Norfolks*

There was of course the usual army rivalry with other battalions that had the temerity to trespass on their 'territory'. The main enemy of the Norfolks were the 1st Battalion, Royal Scots who were billeted just the other side of the Humber. The river may have been the ideal anti-tank obstacle but it could not stop the Scots from paying the Norfolks a 'friendly' visit. The two proud regiments had a bizarre 'mating' ritual.

I'd had a few drinks and I knew there was going to be trouble – the looks and the arguments, I could see it happening. They were tanked up with beer, the Royal Scots, they were good at that! I thought, "I'm going to get out of this!" But I was too late I couldn't get out. All of a sudden somebody threw a gas mask at somebody – "Wallop!" I thought, "Well I've got to join in here, I can't stand here watching!" Punching and kicking and I thought, "Bugger this!" There was a billiard table and I got under it out of the way. It gradually quietened down and it all broke up. They got the police up there, I think the publican phoned them up. We weren't far from the billets and I walked in and when I went to undress I'd got billiard balls in my pockets – I don't know how they got there whether I picked them up to throw them or what! *Private Stan Roffey, Carrier Platoon, HQ Coy, 2nd Norfolks*

Colonel Winter had appointed Sergeant Bert Fitt as his Provost

The Norfolks own dance band. Danny Boast is playing the saxophone on the right.

Sergeant, presumably adopting the tried and trusted principle of setting a poacher to be his gamekeeper. Fitt had been the despair of provost sergeants at several points of his career due to his willingness to defend his own, his friends and his regiment's honour with his hard, proficient fists. Now it was his job to prevent such lapses in discipline. He took to his new role with an enthusiasm that was almost excessive.

I used to turn out the Admiral Hawk every night. My police corporal, and another policeman used to turn out the Granby public house. Both those houses were on the square and that's where you used to get the trouble. The Royal Scots and the Norfolks used to fight like blazes, every night you'd get some of them fighting. The police didn't intervene, what they used to do was come to the sergeants' mess to see if I was there. They used to tell me there's a fight going on in the square, would I go and quieten it down. I'd go and get hold of the first one that was fighting nearest me and I'd sling him in a room for a few hours to quieten them down, put them on a charge and they'd be up the next morning. The Second in Command of the battalion at the time was a chap named Bob Scott. When you marched them into him you'd give your evidence. He used to ask you straight out, "Who was winning?" If you said that the Royal Scott was winning he got punished but if the Norfolk was winning he used to get a rocket and Scott let him get away with it. That was his attitude. *Provost Sergeant Bert Fitt, HQ Coy, 2nd Norfolks*

Fitt took to his new role with a refreshing enthusiasm, almost revelling in the sport of discovering miscreants and bringing the appropriate, if individually stylized, punishments upon them. He patrolled the mean streets of Hessle wearing civilian shoes instead of his iron studded army boots so as not to upset the locals, but also to catch his prospective victims unawares.

Bert Fitt

I was out on patrol one night and I heard the boots come clomp, clomp, clomp along. There shouldn't have been anybody out. So I got in a doorway, stood back and I watched them come up the road – they never spotted me! When they got past me, I stepped out and started following them. Then they took their boots off, tied the laces and slung the boots around their neck. So they were walking in bare stockinged feet. I knew they had got to go down a cinder track. As they stepped their pace up, I stepped mine up and if they broke into a trot, so did I. But I didn't intend catching them up at all – I intended to make them run on this cinder track. They turned onto the cinder track and they ran so far, then just sat down on the side. It was playing their poor old feet up! I went up to them and they said "That's a fair cop sergeant, we can't run on this!" *Provost Sergeant Bert Fitt, HQ Coy, 2nd Norfolks*

His punishment parades soon acquired a reputation second to none. One soldier was unwise enough to complain after one of these sessions that he had not had his three minutes 'at ease' as required in King's Regulations. Fitt demonstrated he was more than a match for this barrack room lawyer at his next punishment parade.

I went up to this chap, I showed him my watch and said "You see the time, you note that?" "Yes Sir!" "Right!" Then I stood him at ease – stood the lot of them at ease. At the end of three minutes, I showed him my watch again, "You've had three minutes stand at ease?" "Yes, sergeant, alright!" Then we started. I went to town on them – for fifty seven minutes non-stop, changing direction every fifth pace. At the end of the fifty seven minutes drill, I went

A group of Norfolk officers.

to the chap and I said "See the watch, you've had fifty seven minutes drill, three minutes stand at ease!" Then I handed them over to the policeman and said "Take them back to the billets". Well the sweat was pouring off of them, they were soaking wet through with sweat. When they got back, of course the older hands they jumped on the chap who made the complaint and told him, "You should have known better than blinking complain against him!" *Provost Sergeant Bert Fitt, HQ Coy, 2nd Norfolks*

While the battalion was stationed at Hessle they were within sight of the ferocious German air raids on Hull. The battalion was a natural reservoir of men to help out the over-stretched emergency services. On one occasion Fitt and a party of men were helping out with the water hoses when a fire started in the timber stacks area of the docks. 'Winkie' became uncomfortably aware that things were hotting up.

Things were getting very warm behind me and I thought it was the heat from the fire that was burning. I was controlling this hose and all of a sudden somebody put a hose on me! I wasn't very pleased but when I put my hand behind to see how wet it was, I just felt bare skin! All my seat of my trousers was all burnt out – I was on fire and didn't know it – they had put the fire out. It was rather embarrassing, because I'd got no seat in my trousers! *Provost Sergeant Bert Fitt, HQ Coy, 2nd Norfolks*

Given what lay behind and ahead of them one task had an ironic flavour of the charnal house.

My platoon was sent on to the docks to get rid of the meat that had been contaminated in a big refrigerated warehouse. All the pipes had burst all over these sides of meat that had come in from the Argentine. It was all rotting and we had to get rid of it, I understand it was going to soap factories. You can imagine all this rotting meat with this ammonia from these pipes. The smell was terrible and of course it affected your legs, the ammonia got onto your feet, right through your shoes, so we bound our legs up with sandbags to keep the ammonia out. I always think it was a bit ironic, we were dealing with all this rotten meat, sliding about off these mountains and putting it onto lorries. Then, when it came to lunchtime we were offered luncheon meat! Nobody could fancy it, nobody could eat – a lot of it went in the dock. *Corporal William Robinson, A Coy, 2nd Norfolks*

Parties of men were also sent to try and clear the roads by shovelling away the rubble from collapsed houses and buildings. There were numerous civilian casualties and inevitably several heart rending sights.

I saw a young girl, 15 or 16, she lay partly on the pavement, her legs on the road and a cycle near. She looked as though she was asleep. I touched the pulse on the left wrist pushing two fingers

90

Destroyed grain silos in the Hull dock area, May 1941.   IWM660

Chaos on the streets of Hull. The Norfolks were called upon to help clear the bomb damage and help rescue buried civilians, June 1942.   IWM ZZZ6909C

down and there was no pulse there. She looked like wax and she was obviously dead but there wasn't a mark on her. I was told it was blast. *Private Dick Fiddament, 2nd Norfolks*

Each company of the battalion put in stints on instant response coastal defence duty.

We were responsible for from Patrington all the way up the coast about 50 mile. We had to take turns in being on duty for 24 hours a day, a group with an officer, senior NCOs and about 30 men in a bus. We had a drill which was to embus and debus in an old bus that had been confiscated – it had no windows in. Most of the 24 hours we spent in the bus and the idea was that if there was a message came through that a landing had been made somewhere we were to go up the coast. Before the bus stopped, it just slowed up and then you had to debus as quickly as possible ie through the windows. That was the idea of having no glass in and we'd rush to take up the positions to hold the enemy who had landed. The idea was keep the enemy at bay. You can just imagine the idea of the lads with a rifle trying to get out of a bus window! *Sergeant Walter Gilding, Mortar Platoon, HQ Coy, 2nd Norfolks*

In January 1941 the battalion was sent for combined operations training aboard HMS *Glenairn* in Loch Fyne. They were one of the first units to try out the new assault and landing craft which were being developed with the long term aim of invading Europe. Scotland in January was not considered the ideal time for such training by the long suffering men.

We were roused at three or four in the morning with klaxons going. You hopped out of your hammock, put your gear on and reported to your station on deck. Then down the scrambling nets into these assault landing craft which were bobbing about down below. That all sounds great fun, but this was in sub zero temperatures. It was bitterly cold, bitterly cold. To create the impression you were way out to sea the assault landing craft would bob around for say 20 or 25 minutes before going into the beach. These flat bottomed boats used to send spray all over you and although we were kitted out with leather jerkins your hands got so cold that you just couldn't even feel the rifle, you held it as though you were nursing a baby! You'd touch down and run up the beach which was at that time covered in 18 inches of snow! We ran 20 yards inland, flopped down on the snow, lay there for 20 minutes or so and then that was the exercise finished. We'd re-embark, back to the ship. By this time you're so bloody cold that when you got aboard the heat would hit you – it'd got to be 80 degrees plus in the ship and after a few minutes all the joints of your hands would start to throb. God! It was so painful! *Sergeant Fred Hazell, D Coy, 2nd Norfolks*

The Bren gun carriers tried out the Landing Ship Tanks. In theory at least they had an easier time of it.

The weather was absolutely freezing. I felt sorry for the chaps that had to wade off the boat on to the shore. They had to run up the hill as hard as they could and take up position. Them poor buggers, half of them were soaking wet, it's a wonder they never got pneumonia. We had to come off the landing craft. Being the officer's carrier I was the first to come off. In these carriers when you do maintenance you undo this plate in the bottom and brush all the dirt through this hole. Some time or other I'd forgotten to put it back and as I came off the boat on to the shore I hit the water. It wasn't deep, but I just hit the water and a spout of water came up this hole which I'd forgotten to cover up. Just like a fountain, right up in the air and down my neck. I knew what I'd done – I thought, "Silly bugger!" *Private Stan Roffey, Carrier Platoon, HQ Coy, 2nd Norfolks*

Back again at Hessle the training continued remorselessly with a

18 Platoon, D Company. Back row: *Beresford, unidentified, Clarke, Colclough, Cousins, Corporal Timber, MaGuire, unidentified, Lance Corporal Landon, Hughs, Bayford.* Middle row: *Coniff, Tomsett, Brown, Bradfield, Bealy, Browne, Derhan, Battley, Lance Corporal Hingley, Hodges, Russell.* Front row: *Corporal Brighton, Corporal Long, unidentified, Corporal Cron, Sergeant Cook, Lieutenant Sargent, Corporal Rolleston, Corporal Hope, Lance Corporal Garrat, Brett.*

A group of Norfolk officers and 4th Brigade staff: Perry, Hatch, unidentified, Brigadier William Goschen, Boldero, the Padre, unidentified, Colonel George Winter, Howard, Twidle, Phillips.

particular emphasis on route marches.

There were very intensive route marches brought about because of the lack of fitness in France. Every other day a ten mile route march in full service marching order – a fair weight. Then it was stepped up to 25 miles a day, twice a week. The final one was a 50 mile march in 24 hours. You were not allowed back in until you got the last man home. That meant the fit ones were carrying two or three rifles, somebody had got the Bren gun and the weak ones were being held up either side by two of the others to get him home. You had to get the whole squad back and you couldn't go into your houses until you'd got the last man back. *Sergeant Fred Rolleston, D Coy, 2nd Norfolks*

Battalion officers taken at Fairford, April 1942. Back row: *Muir, Edrupt, Stopford, Emms, Franses Solomon, Aitkens, Lowe, Whitaker, Blount, Howard, Fulton, Green, Bothway, Davies, Hinde.* Middle row: *Randle, Perry, Phillips, Lynch, the Padre, Twidle, Scott, Winter, Wilkins, Hatch, Swainson, Brown, Grant, Bradshaw, Sargent.* Front row: *Walford, Reynolds, Buckingham, Hornor, Dickson, Kirkland, Roberts, Swainson.*

Various group photographs were taken to commemorate the moment as the Norfolks prepared to go to war.

Colonel Winter may have slightly misjudged the mood of his men as he sought to impress his opposite number in the 1/8th Battalion, Lancashire Fusiliers.

We'd been out for the best part of 24 hours. We'd crept off at the crack of dawn one day, done manoeuvres, and we were due to be transported back to the billets because we were then about 25-30 miles away from our billet. The CO of the Lancashire Fusiliers turned to Colonel Winter and said, "Your men look knackered!" He said, "They're not, I'll prove it to you!" He sent the transport off and we walked back. He was very unpopular all round and this was the sort of typical action one would have expected from him. Had he walked with us I don't think anybody would have complained, but when he drives alongside you in his open wagon that is really irritating. *Sergeant Fred Hazell, D Coy, 2nd Norfolks*

Divisional exercises took place on the Ilkley Moors. Whilst there Private Dick Fiddament took the opportunity to play a simply splendid practical joke which really deserves a wider audience than it initially received in 1941.

There was myself, Jimmy Wright, Alfie Clements, Percy Utting, Tommy Knutt.... Off we tramped down to Ilkley to see if there was any chance of a drink and some cigarettes for the boys who smoked. No luck, but they did say that they had some cider. We had a drop, not much, probably a couple of halves, then we started back to camp. It was getting dusk, a slight drizzle and we cut across the marshes. Jimmy Wright and some of these London boys they hadn't seen a cow in a field. As you know if you cross a meadow where there are cattle they tend to group together. If they see you they're curious, they'll come towards you and nuzzle you – but they wouldn't hurt you – but Jimmy didn't know this! Oh no! We were coming across this field and there was a low mist, a bit ethereal, looks a bit weird and you could see the cattle. Of course me, being evil, I said to Percy Utting, "We'll get old Jimmy going, tell him about the cattle, mention that they're bulls!" Jimmy was plodding along in front, he was a big fellow, "Jimmy", he said, "these bloody bulls they're coming towards us!" Which by then they were! I had said to Percy, "Pass the word discreetly, when we say run, run!" We lumbered forwards, I could run, I was fairly athletic, so could the others but Jimmy – no way! He smoked quite a bit, he was cursing and blinding. "Run Jimmy, run!" These fields had dykes, I didn't know this. When we got close to, you could see a few reeds and the sheen of the water. Of course we ran and jumped, three or four foot. Jimmy he came thumping up and he stopped as soon as he saw the water. He took a quick look round, the cows weren't charging, they were ambling! Of course in his imagination he could see himself being gored to death! "Jump,

Jimmy!" He went back a pace or two and he jumped. Needless to say he didn't make it – he was in it up to his knees. We were falling over, it sounds silly, it certainly doesn't sound like the actions of men who were there to defend their country to the death, but there we go! *Private Dick Fiddament, 2nd Norfolks*

During the various exercises and trials of 1940-1941 the NCOs got to know the long term qualities and limitations of their officers. Some were not just 'wet behind the ears', they were plain incompetent!

We got on pretty well together. I suppose to some degree I carried the man. You don't let these things look apparent. It was all done rather discreetly. He couldn't read a map – he couldn't find his way out of a paper bag which is a bit of a disadvantage when you're an infantryman. We had an exercise laid on for the officers and they were trailed by the sergeants who then had to report back on their performance. Mine came straight out of the company commander's tent and went in the wrong direction right from the very start. That was the sort of thing you had to put up with. You had to say, "Why don't we try going over there for a change..." I'd do it as tactfully as I could. He was courageous but he was the sort of chap you could well imagine leading you all into a disaster. He was not the sort of fellow that I would pin any faith in coming out the other end. *Sergeant Fred Hazell, D Coy, 2nd Norfolks*

However slowly, the more intelligent young officers gradually gained experience and began to form a constructive working relationship with their long suffering platoon sergeants.

He was a nice chap who took me under his wing. He quite obviously recognized a very raw young officer. He knew much more about army ways than I did and he helped me along. The troops knew what was going on, understood it and didn't object to it. They accepted officers as a necessary evil and learnt to work with them. One got to feel those who respected one. Also the distinction between respect for the individual officer as opposed to respect for the rank. I was protected by my rank and whatever I did, within limits, however wrong, in training particularly, I would be supported by my senior officers. But I could tell by the look in the eyes of the chaps if I did something which they thought was a bit off. Rank was there as a fall back, that was all. *Second Lieutenant Maurice Franses, 2nd Norfolks*

The men knew that they were destined for overseas service but the destination remained a secret. Finally they got a substantial clue.

We were issued with tropical kit, that horrible topee, khaki drill shirts, shorts that turned down, socks. We walked along the road from headquarters to our billets loaded with all this gear and they said, "Don't say nothing!" I mean the most naïve person in the world couldn't have failed to see that the unit sometime or other was booked to go overseas. *Sergeant Ben Macrae, Carrier Platoon, HQ Coy, 2nd Norfolks*

Fitt was unhappy to think that he might be posted east again after his earlier years of service with the 1st Battalion in India. He decided to ask Colonel Winter for a transfer.

> I asked him for a transfer and he told me the next morning what regiments were open for transfer, gave me my options where to go, my choice. He named me three regiments, all kilted regiments and I told him I couldn't fancy myself in a skirt. So I'd have to go with the battalion, that's what he wanted and that's what he got too! I wasn't going to wear a kilt. I couldn't do that. *Sergeant Bert Fitt, Provost Sergeant, HQ Coy, 2nd Norfolks*

In December 1941 the battalion were moved to the 2nd Division concentration area around the village of Fairford in Gloucestershire. Many of the men and several of the local women were heartbroken to see them leave Hessle.

> The night we left we were down the Ferryboat and it was funny – all the girlfriends came in that night and they were all crying their eyes out. One of the buglers, Sid, he had two big fat girls crying their eyes out all over him. *Sergeant Ben Macrae, Carrier Platoon, HQ Coy, 2nd Norfolks*

The battalion moved into the grounds of the Palmer estate and the officers took the opportunity to establish a real old style Officers' mess.

> In the war we didn't have mess kit, regular officers might have some tucked away somewhere, but they didn't wear it – we were all in battledress. You would assemble in the ante-room having drinks. In peacetime there were many more rules that I wouldn't know about – you mustn't talk about women, you mustn't talk 'shop'. That sort of thing was very much out – it didn't apply any more. Then the President of the Mess Committee, he was the chap always in charge of dinners and that sort of thing, not the CO, he would hammer on the table and say, "Take your seats, gentlemen!" We all went in, particular guests would be brought in at the end by the CO, but otherwise we just sat where we liked together. The PMC always at one end of the long table, Mr Vice at the other end of the table he was a junior officer. The PMC was always a major, very often the commander of the Headquarters Company, he organized the whole thing. The Mess Staff brought in the food and the wine. We had some silver out, we didn't take any silver abroad. It was a regular dinner. You went on till the PMC would catch the CO's eye or send him little messages saying, "Shall we pack up now?" When he did the PMC rose, then everybody else rose and went back to the ante-room. Then wild games would start. Horses

and jockeys – small chaps like me were always the jockey carried on a larger officer – we just charged around trying to unseat the jockeys! Charging about, somebody would grab me and try and get me off, I would grab another one – it was that sort of thing. An amusing one was where you had to get round the ante-room without putting a foot on the floor. Climbing round hanging on to pictures, mantlepieces, window ledges, to get right round. If you fell, or put a foot on the floor that was a round of drinks. Cossack dancing, I was rather good at that myself, leaping up and down, squatting and dancing with your legs. *Second Lieutenant Sam Hornor, HQ Coy, 2nd Norfolks*

Rumours continued to be rife amongst the men as to the nature of the upcoming overseas posting.

We knew by then we were off somewhere but where we didn't know. Then, as in every army, you get the rumours. We went everywhere from Hawaii, to Iceland, to the North Pole, to the South Pole – you name it we were going! Absolute nonsense. *Private Dick Fiddament, 2nd Norfolks*

After inspections by both the King and Churchill the battalion was finally once more ready for the fray. Partings from loved ones were often traumatic, particularly for those who had young children.

I had a special 72 hour compassionate leave when my baby was born. I went to Wisbech which is the other side of Kings Lynn and saw my wife and child. While I was on that special leave I applied for a further extension of 72 hours so I had six days leave to see my baby. She was three days old when I left... *Sergeant Walter Gilding, Mortar Platoon, HQ Coy, 2nd Norfolks*

Many parents had difficulty in restraining their emotions as their sons finished their embarkation leave.

My father was standing on Paddington Station on the opposite platform, because he wouldn't stay near the train. He was in floods of tears, and the lady next to me in the train said, "Look at that gentleman over there!" I said, "That's my father!" He thought he wasn't going to see me again. *Second Lieutenant Maurice Franses, 2nd Norfolks*

CHAPTER SIX

Passage to India

The Norfolks boarded the former tramp steamer SS *Orbita* at Glasgow. As the men boarded in a seemingly never ending stream it was fairly obvious that space on board would be at a premium. When the Orbita sailed on 15 April 1942 some of the men were aware of the enormity of the step that they were collectively taking.

As we first started off going up the Clyde we were seeing all these dockers, crane men, shipbuilders on the side of the Clyde waving.... I thought, "I wish I was them waving – not me!" *Private Stan Roffey, Carrier Platoon, HQ Coy, 2nd Norfolks*
At least they were not alone on the High Seas.

We were part of the biggest convoy that had ever left the United Kingdom at that time, with troops, ammunition and everything. We had the old battleship *Queen Elizabeth*, a nice impressive looking old granny to have in the middle, a couple of small aircraft carriers – large merchant ships with a sort of lid put on top for landing and taking off aeroplanes, all fairly bogus and a half a dozen destroyers that buzzed round us the whole time. *Second Lieutenant Sam Hornor, HQ Coy, 2nd Norfolks*

Accompanying the Norfolks on the their passage to India the battleship Queen Elizabeth *a reassuring stately lady and flagship of the convoy.* Taylor Library

Everyone suffered from the cramped conditions.

> When arrived on the *Orbita* we wondered where everyone was going because I think the passenger capacity was about 600 and here we were with getting up towards 3,000 on the boat. My personal accommodation was with three other sergeants in a one berth cabin. They'd put another bunk over the top of the single bed and the other two laid on the floor, head to toe. We had one wash basin and that had a crack half way down so when they turned the water on, which was once a day, we had just enough water for half a basin, if it was full up you lost half of it through the crack anyway. The four of us had to wash and shave in this. Then we took it in turns to wash socks or pants or whatever out. That was our accommodation. The lads they fared even worse.
> *Sergeant Walter Gilding, Mortar Platoon, HQ Coy, 2nd Norfolks*

The men were cramped together far below the waves in mess decks where they slept in hammocks, on the mess tables and on the floor. They were fully aware of their impossible situation should the worst happen.

> They had these water tight doors which in the event of being torpedoed they were closed to shut that part off. But they didn't close, you couldn't move them, they were rusted up! Yet you had to have somebody stand there, that was the way the army worked, you couldn't close the bloody door but you had to have somebody stand there! *Private Dick Fiddament, 2nd Norfolks*

As they metaphorically festered far below the water line some could not help but think of U–Boats and torpedoes. Others saw it as an opportunity for 'wit'.

> I lay on the floor for a time and you could hear the 'Boom, Boom Boom' of the propeller. The light would go out at say ten at night. Then you would get some wag say, "Listen!" Then they'd get an ammunition boot and they'd whack, 'CLANNGG' "Bloody torpedo!" *Private Dick Fiddament, 2nd Norfolks*

The boat drill practices to prepare for the worst did not engender confidence and some adopted an essentially fatalistic approach.

> We did have boat drill but the position we were in the boat it would have been impossible for anyone to have got out had there been anything happen. Had there been a hit we were so far down that it's all right in practice saying you hang on to the one in front but you can't do it – I would have thought that it would have been far easier to have saluted, said, "Rule Britannia!" and gone down with it because you would never have got up – it would have been panic. *Lance Sergeant William Robinson, A Coy, 2nd Norfolks*

The extreme overcrowding led to severe logistical problems in feeding troops.

The feeding of the men themselves was the most difficult thing I have ever known. The galley could only cope with that small amount that the boat was supposed to accommodate, so they had 2000 extra to be fed. The cooks were on the go the whole of the time – they had to work in relays. The mess orderlies were doing the same. They called us the 'Q' ship of the division because there was always a queue all the way round to the galley from the mess decks. *Sergeant Walter Gilding, Mortar Platoon, HQ Coy, 2nd Norfolks*

As they passed through the Bay of Biscay they ran into increasingly rough weather.

The boat was actually reeling out of the water, hitting the water as it bounced back – really frightening! The chap who was detailed to get the porridge for our breakfast put it in the tray, a huge tray, rather deep and full up with porridge. In the process of coming down to the deck, the boat did one terrific move and he fell. All the porridge went down on to the stairs, plus the water coming in from the sea and the toilets being blocked up – it was really a mess. Of course we all had a laugh but the chap carrying the porridge wasn't so lucky – he got covered! *Private Stan Roffey, Carrier Platoon, HQ Coy, 2nd Norfolks*

Even if the mess orderlies made it intact, sometimes the choice of menu showed that a cruel and vengeful sense of humour lurked somewhere within the kitchens.

The mess orderlies went to pick up the food and they came down with this main meal – and it was tripe! Boiled tripe. I was supervising the dishing up of this tripe. The men were waiting for their plates to be sent down to them. One of the mess orderlies started to dish it up and he was sick in amongst the tripe. That was the finish for me! I just had to leave them to it. *Sergeant Walter Gilding, Mortar Platoon, HQ Coy, 2nd Norfolks*

In these circumstances the toilet arrangements took on a peculiarly important status.

In the Merchant Navy the toilets are referred to as the 'heads'. There's a row of wooden seats, say a dozen and they are flushed by sea-water. You sit there – there's no embarrassment in the army because every one of you has seen whatever there is to see! You sit

Cape Town and Table Mountain.

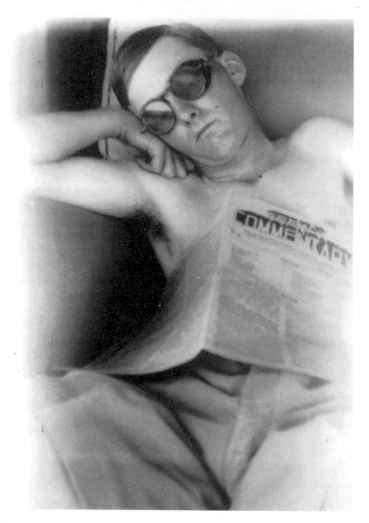

Sam Hornor in relaxed mode.

there and all of a sudden you'd get a swell, the ship will go up and down, port to starboard and all this is slopping about and you'd get a wet backside. *Private Dick Fiddament, 2nd Norfolks*
There were other dangers in using the heads – terrors that could bring a hot flush to the most robust of unsuspecting cheeks.

The toilets were specially made like a steel gully, and that was set up at an angle so that they were continually being flushed by sea water. There were sections and when you used the toilet you just sat and did your business. For a joke somebody would get a piece of newspaper, put it up the top end, set light to it and let it float down whilst somebody was sitting on the toilet. So you had to be careful! *Private Stan Roffey, Carrier Platoon, HQ Coy, 2nd Norfolks*

As they moved into more settled climes and their stomachs settled the men began to take more interest in their surroundings. One frustration was a traditional soldiers' grievance.

There were so many men on board and no women at all! It was a bit hard because one of the very comfortable big liners was within sight on the starboard beam full of WAAFs! All the chaps thought it was most unfair! *Second Lieutenant Sam Hornor, HQ Coy, 2nd Norfolks*

Men began to seek to improve their own lot and sought to escape from the fetid atmosphere below decks.

Once we got out into the hot weather there was no stopping it and I aided and abetted my chaps, I said, "Look, when it gets dark just take your bedroll, go out and sleep on deck – you will at least wash off if we sink instead of being drowned down here!" You couldn't sleep down there, it was hot as hell. So in fact the deck was covered with sleeping chaps every night and nobody said anything because you couldn't in all fairness. *Second Lieutenant Sam Hornor, HQ Coy, 2nd Norfolks*

The sheer lack of space restricted opportunities for effective training but Major Robert Scott improvised as best he could.

Robert Scott used to have battle practice. Chucking old wooden boxes over the side and then he had people with Bren guns to shoot them as though they were on the range. Various NCOs walking about with tent pegs bashing them on the head to simulate battle conditions. It's all part of it – it's cumulative that sort of training. Robert Scott was a great man on this, his philosophy was, "An infantry soldier's no bloody good if he can't shoot straight, because somebody will shoot him first. So Number One object, always, is shooting!" He plugged this like mad – and he was absolutely right! *Second Lieutenant Sam Hornor, HQ Coy, 2nd Norfolks*

After a stop at Freetown where no one was allowed ashore, the convoy steamed on to Capetown.

The first day we stayed in Capetown. Everybody had been asked if they wanted to go on a trip round the town, ladies would be pleased to show them around. That didn't appeal to me, I imagined some little grey haired old lady taking me by the hand and taking me round! So I didn't put my name down, in fact I don't think any of the sergeants did. But when we disembarked there was this whole line of great big open cars all driven by young girls of 17 and 18!!! There was a lot of gnashing of teeth as you can well imagine. *Sergeant Fred Hazell, D Coy, 2nd Norfolks*

After a couple of days the battalion came ashore to Retreat Camp just outside Capetown. The food was in marked contrast to what was available in England.

The food was magnificent. Nobody had seen any fruit and there on the tables was apples, pears, oranges. Mountains of butter, all the sugar you wanted. *Sergeant Fred Hazell, D Coy, 2nd Norfolks*

On 19 May 1942 they left Capetown and finally received news that they and the rest of 2nd Division had been assigned to India.

All the old soldiers that had spent a fair time in India were telling us all that we could expect. They made it sound very attractive. They told us that after ten o'clock in the morning you did nothing, just kept under cover laying on your beds on the verandas. Then maybe you'd do a little bit more from 4.30 onwards. But most of the day was spent at siesta – which appealed to everybody as you can well imagine. I was quite happy because I'd always wanted to go. An uncle of mine had been a district commissioner in India for donkey's years. As a kid we looked at some of his big photograph albums with him standing there with his foot on a tiger's head, his gun across his arms and a whole crowd of beaters behind him. I was delighted at the thought of going to India. *Sergeant Fred Hazell, D Coy, 2nd Norfolks*

CHAPTER SEVEN

Indian Interlude

The Norfolks landed at Bombay on 10 April and moved off immediately by train to Chinchwad Camp. They were not impressed by what they found.

> It was a most desolate looking spot. There wasn't a tree or a bush to be seen anywhere – just the sort of rocky plains running up and down. *Sergeant Fred Hazell, D Coy, 2nd Norfolks*

The men found the Indian climate oppressive in the extreme.

> There was a few parades and I can recall standing to attention in our ranks being inspected. Everyone thought, "My God how long will this last?" I don't know what the temperature was there certainly, 110-120. I do know that we were drinking plenty of liquid and as you drank it you could watch it burst through the pores of your skin. We were literally saturated, you felt just like a limp rag. I don't think we would have been in a fit condition to attack or ward off a five year old child because we weren't acclimatized. *Private Dick Fiddament, 2nd Norfolks*

Another climatic problem was the long brooding monsoon which burst with devastating force on the unprepared Norfolks not long after they had arrived.

> Every night you got thunder and lightning, no rain. Lightning right across the sky, it used to light the place up. We expected rain and they said, "Dig trenches all the way round the tents". We dug little things, one foot, 18 inches, we thought that would be ample! Of course the night it did come down, it laid flat everything in the camp! High wind first, then the rain came down. These little fart-arse trenches they were useless – it just came down in solid sheets of water. The ground got soaked, the pegs pulled out and down came the tents. Everything we had was absolutely soaked. We just stood there, there was nothing we could do about it. There was a sort of fatalistic attitude, "Ah well, it can't get any worse!" You couldn't get any wetter unless you dived in a pool! *Sergeant Ben Macrae, Carrier Platoon, HQ Coy, 2nd Norfolks*

One golden rule of pre-war Indian military life was abandoned in the face of the threat posed by the Japanese who were looming large on the Burmese frontier of India. The 2nd Division were determined to train for war.

> When we got there the training consisted mostly of hardening up. Until we got to Chinchwad, British troops did not march in

A group of immaculate officers with pressed shorts, polished boots and slouch hats at the regulation tilt, with knees nicely turning brown. John Randle, Richard Greene, Richard Bothway, Michael Fulton, Basil Aitken and Gerry Myler.

the heat of the day. But as far as the regiment was concerned they realized that if you were fighting out East, then you may have to fight through the heat of the day and do long marches. So most of the training consisted of route marches, starting off about eight, ten miles and then building up to a matter of about twenty five miles in a day – all in the heat of the day. Very, very hard going. Obviously you had to restrict people drinking water on the line of march, you had to be on the look out for that. You were only permitted to have a sip of water if authority was given from the person in charge of the march. The regiment they did well, they marched everywhere they were asked. Although it was hard going they still did it and the regiment had something to be proud of. They were the first troops to do it. *Provost Sergeant Bert Fitt, HQ Coy, 2nd Battalion, RNR*

Most of the 'old hands' were more amazed than impressed!.

We went on a route march into Poona one day and we got there after mid-day. The people were looking at us saying, "What the hell are these chaps doing out in the mid-day sun!" It was hot! *Second Lieutenant Maurice Franses, 2nd Battalion, RNR*

One problem of acclimatization to Indian conditions of service was dysentery. This could affect even the most august of personages in humiliating, but all too understandable circumstances.

I was standing on guard on the ammunition tent and I was right in front of the RSM's tent. All of a sudden I heard a scuffle, I was looking in front and he was trying to put his trousers on quick. I thought, "Hello, he's got the dysentery! He's going to run!" He came out of the tent, half holding his trousers up and running like hell to go to the latrines – and he didn't make it! He used one of the litter bins for all his mess! Of course I made sure he didn't see me laughing because I would have been well in it! *Private Stan Roffey, Carrier Platoon, HQ Coy, 2nd Norfolks*

Another problem which afflicted almost everybody was prickly heat.

Somebody with a hairy chest would get this prickly heat and it could send you on the verge of bloody insanity. You shouldn't

Sergeant Majors – the backbone of the battalion: CSM Slaughter, CSM Kettle, RSM Wright.

Gerry Myler takes an early bath. Prickly Heat, infections and sores had to be contended with.

scratch, but you did scratch and it would bleed. Then it would become infected and all sore. You'd get it on your head, get it round your private parts – any part of your body. *Private Dick Fiddament, 2nd Norfolks*

On 8 July 1942 a party of 100 men were inspected by the Duke of Gloucester at Poona. The preparations were ludicrous in the extreme.

It was a hand picked squad. We were taken there and then we were actually lifted into our shorts. We had very stiffly starched shorts with beautiful creases. Somebody held them open whilst two others got you under the elbows and put you in like that. Then you buttoned them up. We were picked up by the elbows, carried on to the parade ground and put down in position, Now that takes a bit of whacking doesn't it. While we were standing there somebody came along and gave a little final dust around our toe caps. The Duke of Gloucester whistled down the lines. I don't think he even noticed us! *Sergeant Fred Hazell, D Coy, 2nd Norfolks*

On 10 July the battalion moved to Kharakvasla where a variety of combined operations exercises were carried out until five days later they moved again to Ahmednagar. This was to be their 'home' base for the rest of their stay in India. Most of the men were housed in 'bashas'

The British presence on the streets. Jim Lowe a long way from home.

which were huts constructed from mud and wattle.

We had a long hut which accommodated a company and at the end there was a separate room for the three sergeants. There was a series of these huts and one was divided into five for the five company officers. Then you had stores, the jail, the messes. The buildings were built of single brick up to about three foot. Above

Battley, Hingley, Brown and Bentley in Bombay, 1942.

that would be this sort of raffia work on a timber frame, a tiled roof and mud floors trawled smooth. It dried hard and it was surprising that it didn't dust an awful lot when you think it was just ground you were on. *Sergeant Fred Hazell, 2nd Norfolks*

Their beds were charpoys.

A charpoy is a wooden framed string bed, everybody, all ranks, had charpoys. You first of all had to boil them if they hadn't been used for some time to kill all the bed bugs. Then you stood them in four tobacco tins to stop more bed bugs and other God knows what climbing up! *Second Lieutenant Sam Hornor, HQ Coy, 2nd Norfolks*

There were, however, some of the traditional advantages of serving in India. The men had a large range of Indian servants offering their specialist services of which perhaps the most useful were the dhobi wallah.

> He was an Indian who came round once a week and collected all your shirts and what have you, to take and be laundered. Everything was marked with Indian ink. You had your own sign, dots and dashes. How they worked it out I don't know, but I never knew of anyone who got the wrong kit. They used to take this away and break all the stones in India by bashing them with the clothes, bashing them against the stones. They lay them out to dry in the sun and bleach them. Then they had one of these great big irons with charcoal, they'd iron it all over and it would come back wonderful. *Private Stan Banks, Signals Section, HQ Coy, 2nd Bn RNR*

They had hardly settled in at Ahmednagar when they were sent to the Bombay area for more combined operations training which in the event was cancelled because of serious civil disturbances. The Congress of India had passed the famous 'Quit India' motion and as a result large scale demonstrations were taking place in many of the main conurbations. The Norfolks embarked on a series of marches to 'show the flag' in Bombay.

> We sent out platoons or companies marching round the town in what they called 'flag marches'. We were preceded by four members from the Bombay Police dressed in their natty little uniforms. They had one in the gutter and one in the gutter on the other side of the road, each with a long stick, about seven foot long. Any Indian that got anywhere near us got a clout on the head with the stick. The other two had short canes and were swiping them. We marched through the town with fixed bayonets and carrying our rifles at the port looking all very ferocious. They had the impression that we all had one 'up the spout' but in point of fact we hadn't got any ammunition at all. Good heavens if you'd have fired a round at an Indian there would be a tremendous furore. I suppose we looked pretty fearsome to the natives. *Sergeant Fred Hazell, D Coy, 2nd Norfolks*

On 10 August the battalion was sent to the industrial cotton manufacturing city of Ahmedabad. On their arrival at the railway station they were met by a huge demonstration.

> It was a very big town with a hell of a lot of cotton mills. The sort of town that Hollywood would depict in the films of India. You had this main road, over a mile long, dead straight, and all the buildings on either side. There were alleyways at the road side which would have very ornate wrought iron gates. We came out of

The Norfolks on internal security duties 'showing the flag'.

the station and formed up as a battalion by companies. The entire road as far as you could see was jammed solid with Indians. Jammed solid! Thousands and thousands of them and they were all up on the roof tops saying, "INFIDEL! INFIDEL!" *Sergeant Fred Hazell, D Coy, 2nd Norfolks*
The situation was delicate for although the demonstration was peaceful it was by no means friendly.

On the march. Major Tim Wilkins leading the battalion.

They were young students, younger population and they all wore white linen. A baggy kind of trousers, smock type white linen jacket, some were embroidered some weren't. They had these little white side caps that stood on the top of the head. Among the crowd there were stretchers made out of bamboo and on the stretcher was a corpse. Covered completely over with flowers garlanded all over it. We were told that they and the Indian Police had rioted and one or two of them had been killed. They were displaying these bodies and chanting. The only comparison was to see a football crowd cramming in, a solid mass of people. They're shouting things in Hindustani, Urdu or whatever and you know that if there was the slightest chance they'd crush you like a beetle. You could see the hate in their faces. The abuse, the spitting and that makes you feel awful because its not our nature to be like that – we're not bullies – we weren't Germans, we weren't Nazis. They were taking their spite out on us because of the 'Establishment'.
Private Dick Fiddament, 2nd Norfolks

The battalion was perhaps fortunate that their Second in Command, Major Robert Scott, had served in the Palestine Police and was well used to dealing with demonstrations by use of the minimum of force – although it was rumoured that he would have used as much force as possible were he to follow his personal inclinations.

Captain Fulton was standing in front of the Company with his little cane and Bob Scott came down, looked at this crowd and said, "Fulton, get rid of these people!" Captain Fulton ran at them with his little cane and I have never seen anything like it in my life. There were tens of thousands of them there and they turned and they fled. They knocked over peanut barrows, sweetmeat barrows, people were knocking themselves out on lampposts – it was amazing! *Sergeant Fred Hazell, D Coy, 2nd Norfolks*

The next step was the occupation of Congress House the nerve centre of the Congress Party.

The next day Robert decided to deal with this situation so he had the Motor Transport people take the silencers off the three Bren gun carriers, pack them with men without arms, with lathis and drove them down into the town. Well they made a noise like a tank without a silencer. They went straight to Congress headquarters into which he sent all the troops. Threw anybody down the stairs who got in the way, threw out all the papers, all the bumf, lit a fire outside, burnt all their records, everything. Then he sent for a company to occupy it and a couple of other buildings. That was that. *Lieutenant Sam Hornor, Signal Officer, HQ Coy, 2nd Norfolks*

The situation still remained fraught.

The first night we did a guard, I don't think anyone slept. We were all round this building with fixed bayonets. We had a couple of Bren guns on the roof and in various other places, dispersed in the grounds. They came up to the gate and they were chanting abuse, which we didn't understand anyway! *Private Dick Fiddament, 2nd Norfolks*

The tense atmosphere did not prevent the troops from responding to some of the insults literally thrown at them in English.

There was a wall round this whole building, about an eight foot wall and the Indians were throwing little notes wrapped in a brick over saying, "We're coming tonight to get you all. You'll have your throats slit" This, that and the other. The lads used to get the piece of paper and just write "'Balls!" on it and throw it back. *Sergeant Fred Hazell, D Coy, 2nd Norfolks*

For junior officers this period was extremely stressful as they sought to impose order without using any force and knowing that they would be held directly responsible if anything went wrong.

You knew you would be court-martialled before you started and everyone had heard the story of Dyer and Amritsar. You had a writer who wrote down whatever you said and put this notice up – 'Stop, or I fire' – a civilian magistrate mumbles away and you hope that they stop! I was lucky they always did. The worst thing was in going through the streets because they'd empty rubbish over you. Excreta wrapped up in a piece of newspaper was a good bomb! It wasn't very pleasant. We got an infection which raised

Second Lieutenant Dickie Davies recalls the fine line the Norfolks had to walk in keeping civil order among a people who hated the British presence in India.

terrible sores, great purple sores. *Second Lieutenant Dickie Davies, D Coy, 2nd Norfolks*

Nevertheless a 'flash point' having been avoided, eventually everything calmed down and order was restored by the beginning of September when they were relieved of their duties and returned to Ahmednagar. They even got a send off from Indian civilians on leaving.

> We marched down the whole length of the town to the station and practically the whole population turned out and cheered us. In the local newspaper there was an article which gave a very good account of us saying we were a very fine disciplined regiment. What started off looking like a pretty tricky operation ended up very friendly. *Sergeant Fred Hazell, D Coy, 2nd Norfolks*

The next year was spent in various forms of specialized training in combined operations and jungle warfare. Ahmednagar was the base but the battalion moved to various venues to hone their skills. River crossings using toggle ropes and boats; extensive treks through rough country; co-operation exercises with armoured formations; and full scale assault craft landings – all endlessly practised. Jungle training was given special emphasis with the battalion moving to the Belgaum area. Here the men were put through a reaction firing assault course whereby they would creep through a jungle area as if in action. All around them were pop-up targets.

D Company at Ahmednagar.

They were operated by virtue of somebody behind pulling a string or wire – and up would shoot a target. No sooner was it up than it was down again. Several targets would come up, you were all in a group, you'd be walking along waiting for the next target to come up. Perhaps the chap next to you he'll hit the target. 'Winkie' Fitt was behind you and if you missed he'd fire a revolver past your ear. Not at you, but the noise would make you jump and learn you that you'd got to shoot at this target. They were looked at afterwards to see how many shots were on target. You'd be going on and on and then you'd get to a place where you had to go up a hell of a hill. You'd got to run up there, pretend the Japs were up there and you'd got to charge. Run up there and charge. You were literally out of breath. *Private Stan Roffey, Carrier Platoon, HQ Coy, 2nd Norfolks*

In July 1942 Colonel George Winter gave up the command of the battalion as a result of an attack of malaria and Robert Scott was promoted to replace him. Winter's eccentricities had become a little more marked in India, perhaps because of the heat!

Now George there was at his worst. He used to go round the camp picking up little pieces of paper and if he found a cigarette carton he would put his initials on it, 'GHW' and the date and time. Then he'd come creeping along a week or two afterwards to see if it was still there. Silly old sod! *Captain John Howard, Intelligence Officer, HQ Coy, 2nd Norfolks*

Nevertheless during his time in command a new battalion had been forged from the veritable wreck he had taken over when he arrived at Driffield. Winter was a hard working conscientious officer whose eccentricities merely overshadowed an underlying military competence which many of his officers appreciated.

A brilliant administrator but he found it difficult to liaise with

Colonel Robert Scott.

people. He trained the battalion to a first class standard. He and Robert couldn't have gone to war together because George dithered and Robert didn't. They were both sound soldiers, but that was the way they worked. George would want everybody's stockings tied up in the same way before he attacked. They couldn't have done it together. They would each have done quite competently though in their own way. Everything George did was with the right intentions and it worked – Robert inherited a perfectly trained machine. Without George, Robert wouldn't have succeeded. *Lieutenant Dickie Davies, D Coy, 2nd Norfolks*

The elevation of Robert Scott had an immediate impact on the battalion officers.

The battalion came to life. Here was a person we could in a way identify with, he made us interested in what we were doing, he somehow tolerated bad behaviour and was able to distinguish between pranks and real wrong doing. *Second Lieutenant Maurice Franses, 2nd Norfolks*

Training had always been competitive but Scott raised the tempo still further as he strove to perfect the battalion.

He pitted one person against another, or in my case, one detachment of mortars against another. Going into action, if it took three minutes to mount a mortar, then another detachment would try and beat it, that was the competitive spirit. The same thing with the riflemen firing rapid, so many in such and such a time. To put man against man. All sorts of individual efforts, then it went on to section. A section would go through the jungle to a certain spot in a certain way and time. They would compete against other sections. So it was with sections, platoons and companies working in that competitive way. *Sergeant Walter Gilding, Mortar Platoon, HQ Coy, 2nd Norfolks*

Scott was obsessed with improving the overall standard of marksmanship and he introduced a new competition ribaldly known as the 'swinging tit'.

He had a shell, solid anti-tank shot swinging on the end of a wire, about 200 yards away – you had to hit that. You had to time the swing and get it. I could get four out of five. *Sergeant Ben Macrae, Carrier Platoon, HQ Coy, 2nd Norfolks*

The change in Colonel meant that the battalion had some new ideas in every department!

If you could have got it we would have drunk beer, but we didn't get very much! The Indian gin and whisky were pretty frightful. The gin we thought least lethal was called Carew's. We drank it as a long drink – not neat. There was a famous invention of Robert Scott – gin and onion. That was typical of Robert. We

Battalion cross country team. Dickie Davies in at the back on the left.

Grenade tossing event. Major Roger Twidle (with his left foot clearly over the line) caught in the act of throwing, under the critical gaze of Major Henry Conder.

Inventive and unusual events were thought up to test the strength and skills of the Norfolks: here a competition is underway to wind up a weight on the end of a piece of string – not as easy as it looks!

The sports day over and Major-General Grover awards the prizes.

The battalion boxing team with the 2nd Division trophy.

hadn't got any bitters to put with the gin so Robert said, "We will try onions – I always used to use onions with gin in Palestine!" So all the subalterns used to drink gin and onion. Not at all bad, you should try it one day! *Captain John Howard, Intelligence Officer, HQ Coy, 2nd B, RNR*

The battalion had a new issue of Lee Enfield rifles during this period. Hazel and two others were given the task of zeroing the whole of D Company's rifles with the assistance of an armourer.

You'd fire five rounds and you were expected to get five rounds in a group about two inches across. It didn't matter where they were on the range, they could be right up the top left hand corner, but you'd then tell the armourer where they were. He would then adjust the sights to bring it in the bull. You then fired another five and only when you'd got five in the centre of the bull was the rifle then considered correct. Amongst these there was one – the woodwork was beautiful, it didn't require any adjustment and its number was double seven, double seven, double seven. I thought to myself, "Good heavens alive – that's for me!" I put it aside and when it went to the stores I said to the storeman, "When these are issued that's the one I want!" And I got it! So when I was given a

Privates Evans and Shaw with their newly zeroed rifles – they were now ready to face the Japanese.

Sten gun and I had to part with this blessed rifle I gave it to Corporal Brighton. I said, "You can look after this for me, but I'm going to want it back", which I did, when we got to Burma I had it back off him. *Sergeant Fred Hazell, D Coy, 2nd Norfolks*

The Sten was a cheap sub-machine gun which was mass produced, reputedly at a cost of only ten shillings each. Many of the men harboured reservations about the reliability of this weapon.

If you banged the butt of a Sten gun you could almost guarantee that what would happen is the bolt, or the bolt head which holds the firing pin, if you banged it, it was so cheaply made and the spring was so weak, that it would come back so far, go forward again, and fire the round. So really speaking there was always the element of risk of somebody getting killed. *Provost Sergeant Bert Fitt, HQ Coy, 2nd Norfolks*

By the start of January the battalion had been together for three-an-a-half years of solid training and in that time it had forged a new identity. Although named the 2nd Battalion Royal Norfolks its character had mutated into a hybrid of regular, territorial and conscript, as indeed happened to so many battalions in the Second World War. They were by that time ready for action which was perhaps just as well as during 1943 the Japanese had been building up their strength in Burma. It was becoming obvious that at some point in 1944 they would launch an assault on the jewel in the British Imperial crown – India. Neverthe-

Cook Sergeant Larkin with something more exotic than the men usually got.

less, although the overall British policy was defensive, Admiral Lord Louis Mountbatten, as the Supreme Allied Commander in the South East Asia Command was keen not to adopt too supine a posture. The 2nd Division was therefore specially trained in combined operations with a view to striking back at the Japanese wherever possible. The first possibility seriously considered were the Andaman Islands but the greater strategic picture demanded the return of many of the specialist landing assault craft to England in readiness for the D Day invasion of Europe. Not willing to give up, Mountbatten initiated planning for a less ambitious assault behind the Japanese lines on the Mayu Peninsula with

The men of Maurice Franses' platoon take a communal bath.

A serious towel shortage! Richard Greene, Richard Bothway, Gerry Myler and Maurice Franses.

the aim of cutting off and isolating the Japanese 55th Division. Once again the primacy of the European campaign confounded Mountbatten and in January 1944 this too had to be abandoned as the rest of the landing craft were recalled. The mortified Commander-in-Chief began a tour of the 2nd Division to meet as many of the men as possible to explain to them why once again, they were being thwarted from a chance of striking at the Japanese. He reached the Norfolks on 21

D Company take to the High Seas on a trip to Goa. Major Dennis Hatch is kneeling with the moustache.

January 1944.

Mountbatten decided to visit us, knowing how sad everybody would be at missing this expedition. Nobody actually told him that a lot of the chaps had said, "That's good – didn't like the sound of that much!" He wanted to speak to the troops and he was a very difficult chap to manage because he would not have troops paraded to speak to. All he wanted was a soapbox! You had to have a soapbox for him to stand on and then they clustered round him and he addressed them. It is much more difficult to arrange something like that than having just an ordinary proper parade. The RSM was not supposed to rehearse the battalion but nevertheless, he thought he'd better! The soapbox was found and put out ready. Then the battalion was hidden behind all the huts. The RSM said, "Now you mustn't march but you've got to go round that box! So when I shout, 'SAUNTER!' – you SAUNTER!!!" The battalion then had to practise sauntering out and getting round a soapbox – it was very funny watching it!

Lieutenant Sam Hornor, Signal Officer, HQ Coy, 2nd Norfolks

Mountbatten's informal approach, however phoney and posed, struck a chord with many of the men used to Generals and minor royalty inspecting them with their noses in the air. By this time Fitt had been assigned as a platoon sergeant with B Coy.

When he came onto the parade ground, he just called them, and of course they were all hid up behind the company lines. They just marched on and halted, turned inwards and he just beckoned them forward, told them to close in on him. He said "I know very well that you want to know what bastard put you on all this extra training, well come forward and have a look at him!" *Sergeant Bert Fitt, B Coy, 2nd Norfolks*

Sergeant Gilding, for one, was an exceptionally keen soldier who was inspired by Mountbatten's address.

He just gave us a talk

Lord Louis Mountbatten.

131

saying that we would reap the benefits from all this training, and possibly it wouldn't be long before we were called upon to carry out the job that we were intended to do. I think everybody got to a pitch where it was like a boxer – you train up to a certain pitch and then if it doesn't come off you slump back with disappointment. I think everybody was raring to go and to have it knocked on the head was a little bit of a disappointment. More than a little bit. *Sergeant Walter Gilding, Mortar Platoon, HQ Coy, 2nd Norfolks*

Norfolk officers ready for the 'off'!

CHAPTER EIGHT

The Battle for Kohima

In the event the Norfolks did indeed not have long to wait until the Japanese launched their offensive which was intended to burst out of Burma to seize control of the crucial British base at Imphal in the Indian border state of Manipur. On 6 February their 55th Division Group started a diversionary offensive in the Arakan with the intention not only of destroying the British forces there, but of sucking in any reserves which might otherwise reinforce the Imphal Plain. The main Japanese attacks on Imphal began in early March as their 33rd Division attacked towards Tildum, the 15th Division thrust towards Imphal whilst the 31st Division was given the task of capturing Kohima. Although the British Fourteenth Army Commander, Major-General Sir William Slim, was caught a little on the hop by the timing, he had already made the wise command decision that the 17th and 20th Indian Divisions would fall back to the Imphal Plain where they would join the 23rd Indian Division to create a self contained defensive block. This would be re-supplied if necessary by air whilst the Japanese would have a long and tortuous line of communications with all the problems that that entailed. However Slim had not correctly divined the serious nature of the Japanese threat to Kohima and beyond it the major supply centre of Dimapur. As a result the only troops defending the crucial position of Kohima when the Japanese arrived in strength on 4 April 1944 were a scratch garrison force distributed on a series of hills and spurs which together formed the Kohima Ridge.

The original defensive positions were located on IGH Ridge, Garrison Hill, the environs of the District Commissioner's Bungalow, Kuki Picquet, FSD Hill, DIS Ridge, Jail Hill and GPT Ridge. The first contact was made in the area of Aradura Spur on the evening of 3 April (see map p 143). From then on events moved with bewildering speed. By the morning of 5 April the elite Japanese 58th Regiment had established itself in the area of the Naga Village, in the afternoon GPT Ridge had been seized and next morning they over-ran the

General Sir William Slim

133

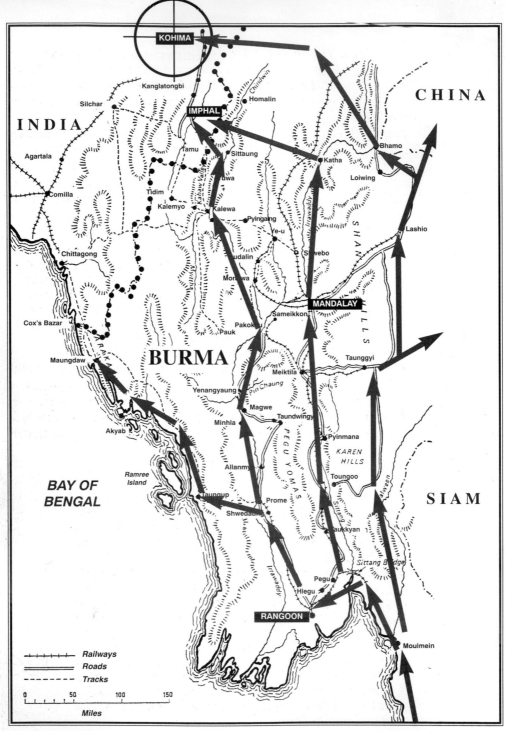

General situation map showing Burma in relation to India and Kohima. By the time the Norfolks reached northern India in April 1944 the Japanese were at Kohima, after having conquered Burma.

defensive positions on Jail Hill. It was fortunate indeed that on 5 April the clearly inadequate garrison force was stiffened by the arrival of 1/4th Battalion, Royal West Kents which was part of 161 Brigade. The rest of 161 Brigade was established in a box at Jotsoma some three miles from Kohima itself.

Nevertheless it was obvious that the situation was desperate and the British 2nd Division was ordered up to the Kohima front. When the movement orders arrived the 2nd Norfolks had recently completed another period of jungle training in Belgaum and had moved to Bangalore. Many of the men had been sent to the local hill stations on local leave. They were recalled in haste and last minute preparations were made in extreme secrecy.

> We were all told that we were not to mention anything about what might be happening. The 2 Div signs had to be taken off all vehicles - but the strange thing is afterwards, after all this hush hush business, it apparently had been given out that the Japanese said that they had heard that the crack 2nd British Division were bound for Kohima, Imphal. It was a bit of a laugh in the battalion that eveything was all 'hush hush' yet the Japanese knew all about it. *Sergeant Walter Gilding, B Echelon, 2nd Norfolks*

The battalion moved the 875 miles by rail to Amada Road near Calcutta where they found they were to be transported by air for the next 600 miles to the divisional concentration area at Dimapur which they reached by 10 April 1944. They were flown in battered Dakotas and Commandos provided by the Americans. Sam Hornor was quite frankly nonplussed.

> We were going to be flown in – the one thing we'd never practised! We'd practised moving in every other conceivable way except in aeroplanes. So we'd got to work out load tables for all our kit, our specialist kit and everything that would fit on a Dakota. We were given the load that a Dakota would carry, then we had to work everything out. Well we tried, I mean how much does a wireless set weigh? I didn't know what anything weighed, but we all sort of got there in a vague way, very vague I might say! I said, "Sergeant White, you and I and two other signallers will go on our plane with all our wireless sets, the batteries and all the things that we really must have and we'll stick with them – to hell with the rest!" That didn't make anything like a plane load and the rest of it was made up with reserve 3" mortar ammunition – I thought that was an unfortunate choice – if we crashed it would be the most magnificent explosion! *Lieutenant Sam Hornor, Signal Officer, HQ Coy, 2nd Norfolks*

Sam Hornor

Dakotas were the only means of of rushing up reinforcements and suplies to the beleagured Indian frontier. IWM IND3402 & 5277

The men found it an interesting experience as they sat on the rough seats almost all of them flying for the first time.

> We had to go over a range of hills to get to Dimapur, and you would be flying along quite happy. All of a sudden the plane would just drop, as though it was dropping out of the sky. It would go down about, oh some twenty, thirty feet, more than that and your heart used to come up to your mouth. Then you'd drop down in these valleys and of course then away you'd go again. There was no danger to it, not as far as we knew. But it was rather a thrill. *Sergeant Bert Fitt, B Coy, 2nd Norfolks*

What they did notice was the omnipresent jungle far below them.

> You just couldn't believe it. The thing that was going through everybody's minds was, "Where the bloody hell are we going to land?" It was just like the sea only green! *Private Dick Fiddament, 2nd Norfolks*

When they did land they found that it was chaos as usual with order and counter-order leading as usual to disorder.

> Somebody came round with a box of tracer ammunition. Everybody was given a few of these and we were told to put one for every three bullets in the magazines of the Bren guns. So everybody was busy loading these up and just when we finished a message came round, "One in every five!" They obviously hadn't got enough to go round. So the whole lot were emptied and we put one in five! Having completed that around came the message, "One in seven!" So they kept us going all night. Dear oh dear! *Sergeant Fred Hazell, D Coy, 2nd Norfolks*

By the time they arrived the situation on the Kohima Ridge had further deteriorated. The Japanese had not only invested the garrison, but also cut off the 161 Brigade box centred on Jotsoma. Major-General John Grover commanding the 2nd Division gave Brigadier Victor Hawkins of the 5th Brigade the task of leading the way, charged with opening the road to Jotsoma. They had already set off first and had come into contact with the Japanese in the Zubza sector. Behind them the 4th Brigade, including the Norfolks, began the move up to Priphema, which was some 28 miles along the Dimapur/Kohima road. John Howard had been appointed as Intelligence Officer to the whole of the 4th Brigade but he still kept up his close links with the Norfolks.

> I have never before or since been so excited in my life; the impression that the whole business was yet another exercise was hard to shake off. Jack Randle, as bored as ever to outward appearance, was as keen as mustard with B Coy. He too still had difficulty in believing that he was not on an exercise, being doubtful whether he should demolish some buildings that

John Howard

obscured his line of fire. The Brigadier reassured him that he could do as he wished in the matter.[6] *Captain John Howard, Intelligence Officer, HQ, 4th Brigade*
After training so hard, for so long, this kind of reaction was difficult to avoid.

It was an interesting commentary on one's training. Always clear up afterwards, make sure everything is neat and tidy, don't leave any rubbish anywhere where you've been, hand in all the spare equipment that you haven't used. Until I realized how different it was, it struck me that there was stuff all over the road, signals stores, all sorts of things just dumped and left – nobody had cleared anything up. Terrible mess everything was in, I thought this was disgraceful, that was my immediate reaction, "How disgraceful this is!" *Lieutenant Sam Hornor, Signal Officer, HQ Coy, 2nd Norfolks*

The Norfolks also made the acquaintance of the Naga villagers who inhabited the area. The Nagas had a strongly developed cultural identity but, to British eyes, they appeared primitive.

They were very fierce looking little chaps but very friendly. Everybody dressed the same, but when I say dressed, it was nothing more than a little apron at the front and an even smaller one hanging round the back. Most of them had a big ivory bangle on their arm. One or two of them had bones through their noses.

British troops in the ubiquitous Bren carriers advancing up the Dimapor Kohima Road. The carriers were little use in the mountainous jungle on either side of the roads, which were little more than tracks.

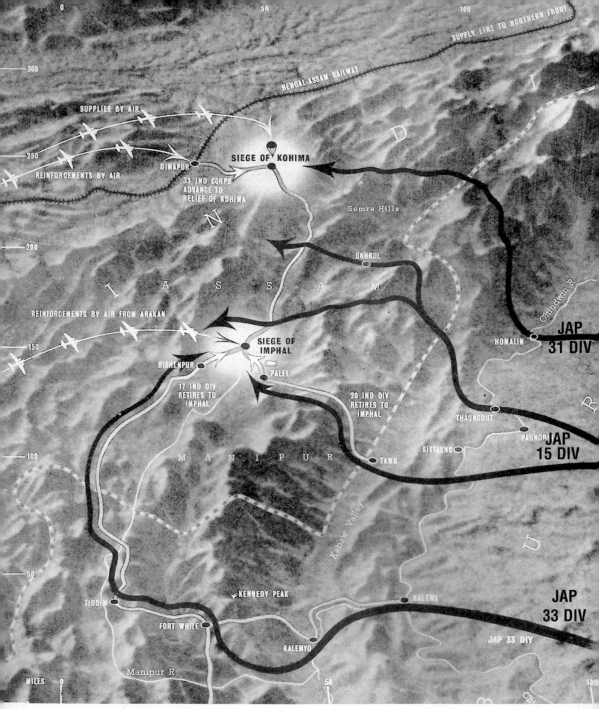

The last bid of the Japanese to capture India. Advancing with great speed three divisions of around 100,000 men swept across the border between Burma and India and invested Imphal and Kohima. Here the decisive battles were fought.

The Dimapur Kohima Road was the life line along which all reinforcements, stores and munitions had to pass. It was also the way the ambulances got the wounded back. It was a busy road. IWM IND3418

They all wore, rather strange, just below the knee, elephant hair, sort of tight and then slackened off, so that when they walked it bounced up and down. They pierced their ears at a young age. I don't know what they used to put in them before we arrived, but while we were there it was a rolled up Woodbine packet about an inch and a quarter in diameter poked through each ear. They carried a spear and a machete. They were so fit because every step they took was either up or down, so their calf muscles were huge, just like rugby balls, that's no exaggeration! They were tremendously fit. They lived very primitively. The villages on the side of the road were a little bit more modern – some of them had roofs made out of flattened tin cans used for tiles, walls would be nothing other than bits of timber and straw – anything they could lay their hands on. But once you got off the road and deeper into the hills it was like going back a thousand years. It was quite incredible. *Sergeant Fred Hazell, D Coy, 2nd Norfolks*

Naga villagers came into the British positions away from the invading Japanese. IWM IND3415

Meanwhile on Kohima Ridge, despite the frequently heroic efforts of the seemingly tireless garrison troops, the Japanese had been able to establish themselves not only on Jail Hill and GPT Ridge but had also captured DIS Ridge on 13 April. Slowly but surely the perimeter was shrinking in the face of wave after wave of determined attacks all along the over-stretched and often overlooked British lines. For the Norfolks the much awaited first contact with the Japanese came at dawn on 14 April. Sergeant Hazell had been ordered on a detached assignment to escort tanks up to the advanced 5th Brigade positions at the village of Zubza.

That evening just as we had stopped and were moving off the road into a small village, Bob Scott was on the wireless set. He came off and he looked around, I stood head and shoulders above everybody else and he said, "HAZELL! Come here!" I went over to him and he said, "I've got a job for you this evening, three tanks are wanted for an assault tomorrow morning by the 5th Brigade.

Fred Hazell

They'll be coming here and I want you and your platoon to escort them up to the 5th Brigade, hand them over and come back at first light. So I said, "Right, Sir!" *Sergeant Fred Hazell, D Coy, 2nd Norfolks*

Hazell's men piled into two trucks and they accompanied the antiquated looking tanks in the pitch dark along the tortuous road.

As we got closer and closer you could hear the sounds of gunfire and grenades going off. Then somebody bobbed out with a torch, flashed it and we pulled up. He said to me, "Put the tanks in there". There was a little bit of flat ground, about the only bit of flat ground I saw in the whole time we were there, about the size of a football pitch. I put the tanks in the form of a triangle, well and truly spread about. But this little fellow didn't tell us where everybody was – he just disappeared. So there we were with no knowledge of where the Jap was

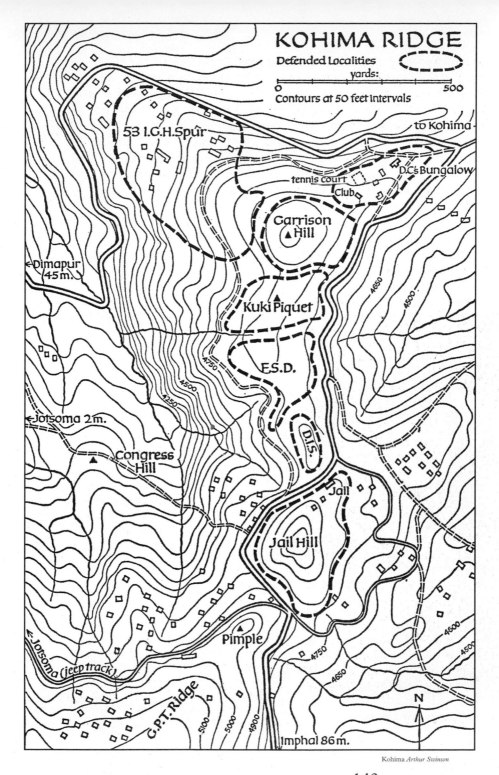

KOHIMA RIDGE

Defended Localities
yards:

0 500

Contours at 50 feet intervals

to Kohima

53 I.G.H. Spur

D.C's Bungalow

tennis court

Club

Garrison
▲ Hill

Dimapur
45 m.

Kuki Piquet ▲

F.S.D.

D.I.S.

Jotsoma 2 m.

Congress
▲ Hill

Jail

Jail Hill

Pimple ▲

Jotsoma (jeep track)

C.P.T. Ridge

N

Imphal 86 m.

Kohima *Arthur Swinson*

Panaoramic view of the Kohima hills. Difficult terrain in which to wage war and certainly not suited to the employment of tanks. IWM 3410

or where the 5th Brigade was! Having stuck the tanks out in a triangle I put a section round each tank. We hadn't dug in up to that stage, we'd had no reason to dig in. Of course having come up into the battle area we should have dug in, but we didn't dig in – that was my first mistake! *Sergeant Fred Hazell, D Coy, 2nd Norfolks*
Very early next morning a corporal reported that he had seen a party of Indians moving in the trees. Hazell was instantly curious.

I said, "Oh! How'd you know they're Indians?" He said, "Well, I couldn't understand what they were saying!" I said, "I'll come and have a look!" I quite casually got up and strolled the length of this area, climbed up the slope into the trees. By that time it was broad daylight. I heard voices on my left and coming towards me, not more than 30 yards away, was an Indian of the Assam Rifles. He was talking over his left shoulder so he was looking away from me. When I looked there was a bloody great Jap officer, big broad fellow and behind him I could see all these little hats bob-bobbing up and down. Then of course, just to cap it all, I realized I'd left my rifle behind! Dear oh dear! The thoughts that passed through my head at that moment – I thought, "My God, you've got a short war, laddie!" I couldn't stay there because they would pass within two feet of me, so I kept one eye on them and one eye sort of swivelling down to the ground as I walked backwards. I didn't want to tread on any twigs and alert them. *Sergeant Fred Hazell, D Coy, 2nd Norfolks*

On reaching the tank laager Hazell warned his troops, though he was frustrated to find that the tank crews couldn't do anything in a hurry because they were all wrapped up in their bedding fast asleep under the tanks.

I was thinking there was nine of them at that stage. I said, "Nobody fire until I give the word". I got my rifle and waited for the 'nine' to appear. It became nine, ten, eleven, twelve, thirteen, fourteen, fifteen, sixteen, seventeen.... In the end we had a hundred of them lined up. As the first one started to disappear from view into the woods again I fired and everyone then joined in with rifle and Bren guns. *Sergeant Fred Hazell, D Coy, 2nd Norfolks*

In fact not everyone opened up for one man's personal courage failed him.

On 'Day One' you could tell those you could rely on and those you couldn't rely on. I had a Bren gunner six foot away from me in a monsoon trench and he never fired a shot. I said to him, "Give me that gun!" Expecting that he would run out and give it to me, but he never budged. I went and grabbed it off him and ran back into my little slot, only to find that he hadn't even got a magazine on it. So I said, "Pass me the magazine!" He just threw them out and they landed in between us. He was grey. In the end I said, "Go down on the road and watch the road to make sure that nobody pinches the trucks". Well I think the road was pretty safe so I got him out of the way. I think he was very grateful. *Sergeant Fred Hazell, D Coy, 2nd Norfolks*

This though was an isolated case, for most of the men opened up with a will on the Japanese fighting patrol.

After the first few shots they dived into the trees and returned the fire. The whole exchange of fire must have lasted about an hour and then it petered out. I had three of the lads hit. We had no idea of how many we'd killed. Someone from 5th Brigade was aware of what was going on and had sent for the ambulances. The three wounded were taken away. One of them had been wounded in France, during the retreat to Dunkirk he got shot in the backside. As he passed me on his stretcher he sort of sat up, beamed at me and said, "I've been shot in the arse again!" I wondered if it was his custom to stick his arse in the air to get it shot at. *Sergeant Fred Hazell, D Coy, 2nd Norfolks*

The new 'veterans' returned to the main unit.

Sitting on the roadside was the Colonel with the Brigadier. The moment the trucks pulled up his batman came rushing over and said, "Bob, wants to have a word with you!" I thought to myself, "Crumbs! Now what have I done wrong!" I went over to him and he said, "Where the bloody hell have you been?" I said, "Well we ran into a little bit of trouble..." He said, "I know, I've had it all, chapter and verse, on the telephone!" I thought I'd better tell him, I said, "I lost three men wounded". He said, "Do you know how many you killed." I said, "No!" He said, "Thirty four – I call that bloody good odds!" *Sergeant Fred Hazell, D Coy, 2nd Norfolks*

For the next few days the battalion carried out a programme of daytime patrols in their vicinity checking for evidence of Japanese infiltration. Although some minor skirmishes were reported most of these were uneventful, although valuable in terms of gaining experience in active service conditions.

The 5th Brigade found progress difficult but succeeded on 15 April in breaking through to the 161 Brigade box at Jotsoma. Meanwhile the perimeter of the beleagured garrison contracted again as by sheer brute strength the Japanese burst through across FSD Hill and straight across to grab Kuki Picquet during the night of 17 April. All that remained was Garrison Hill, the hotly disputed area around the DC's bungalow and IGH Spur. This however marked the high water mark of the Japanese success. The very next day the artillery of 2nd Division began pummelling the Japanese lines while a column of tanks accompanied the 1/1st Punjab Regiment as it forced its way along the road into the perimeter. Although the road was briefly opened, Japanese units were still present in considerable strength in the hills and valleys running down from the Merema Ridge between Zubza and Kohima. Yet the Punjabi reinforcements revitalized the garrison just as they were about to fall. Furthermore the Commander of the Japanese 31st Division, Lieutenant-General Kotuku Sato, was starting to come under increasing pressure from his own superior officers. The Japanese 15th Division had failed in its initial attempts to break into the Imphal box and Lieutenant-General Renya Mutaguchi in command of the 15th Army called upon Sato to send a regimental group of three battalions with supporting artillery to support the 15th Division in their next attack on Imphal. Hence for the rest of the fighting in the Kohima area a subtle, but crucial, sub-text existed as Sato struggled with his twin responsibilities of taking the Kohima Ridge and reinforcing the even

All that remained of the Commissioner's bungalow and the tennis court.
IWM IND3482 and 3483

more strategically significant Imphal offensive. Although Sato appears
initially to have intended to carry out Mutaguchi's orders, he was fatally
undermined by the sheer bloody-minded resistance of the remnants of
the Kohima garrison.

The Japanese attacks continued on the Kohima Ridge as the two
sides slugged it out in a situation where the former DC's tennis court
became a serious objective much coveted by both sides. On 20 April
1/4th Royal West Kents were relieved by the 1st Royal Berkshires and
the 2nd Durham Light Infantry, both from the 6th Brigade. Still the
Japanese flung themselves forward culminating in a final all-out attack
on 23 April which, in a sign of Sato's increasing desperation, used the
battalions supposedly earmarked for Imphal. The Durhams were

pressed hard almost to breaking point on Garrison Hill but held on and inflicted heavy casualties on the Japanese. This marked a sea change as the Japanese priority changed from capturing the rest of the Kohima Ridge to keeping what they had – from an offensive to defensive posture. Attacks and counter-attacks were still made but Sato was increasingly worried by the absence of supplies and ammunition and he henceforth considered his primary role as being to prevent any Allied advance along the Kohima road to break into and relieve the Imphal box. Even more significantly he made no move to send the promised regimental group to assist Mutaguchi's attack on Imphal. The battle for Kohima was inextricably linked with the battle for Imphal. The initiative had clearly passed to the British. But was the 2nd Division strong enough to seize it?

Garrison Hill.   IWM IND3697

CHAPTER NINE

Operation Strident

Major-General John Grover, the commander of the 2nd Division, was not without his own problems as he faced up to the difficult task of ejecting the Japanese from their strongpoints in the Kohima area. Grover's immediate senior, Lieutenant-General Montagu Stopford, commanding the XXX Corps, was, in the manner of senior officers the world over, fairly unsympathetic to the problems Grover was facing and on 24 April came forward to tell him so in person. In brief: the 6th Brigade were fully engaged in holding the vital perimeter positions on the Kohima Ridge; the 5th Brigade were faced with an extraordinarily difficult task in clearing the Merema Ridge towards Naga Village south of the Kohima Road; while the 4th Brigade had replaced the 161st Brigade in the Jotsoma box area. To complicate the situation Grover had recently become aware that Japanese formations of uncertain strength were operating in the foothills of Mount Pulebadze to the north of the Kohima road and generally south west of the Kohima Ridge. Given the natural defensive strength of the Assam country and the Japanese genius for the construction of interlocking defensive positions it was obvious that either a good deal more troops or considerable tactical skill would be required to break the stalemate. Grover's response was audacious indeed. A frontal attack would be suicidal so instead he sought to move round the Japanese southern flank. The 4th Brigade, commanded by Brigadier William Goschen, less

Major-General John Grover

151

the 1/8th Lancashire Fusiliers, were to launch a right hook behind Pulebadze, down on to Aradura Spur to cut the road linking Kohima to Imphal, in other words to establish themselves right across the Japanese lines of communication. To lead the way the brigade was assigned the 143rd Special Service Company under Major McGeorge. The risks of this manoeuvre, code named 'Operation Strident' were obvious and it probably would not have been attempted in normal military circumstances. The country was mountainous in the extreme with Pulebadze standing proudly at no less than 7,522 feet. This perhaps would not have been such a problem if its slopes had not been slashed by a myriad of steep gullies tumbling down covered in thick and what was, by any conventional wisdom, impassable jungle. It was hoped that the very unfeasibility of the operation would be its own protection.

If surprise was the objective then the initial omens were certainly fair, with the Norfolks themselves caught completely on the hop by their sudden orders to march 'into the green'. Lieutenant Colonel Robert Scott was actually engaged in a series of reconnaissances in case the battalion was called from reserve to take part in an attack. It was only on his return at 1400 that his second in command, Major Henry Conder, was able to tell him that the battalion had been given new orders.

> Robert Scott called an 'O' Group. The order group would be the CO and his TAC Headquarters complete, the intelligence officer, the signal officer. Then all the company commanders, all the specialist platoon commanders, mortars and so on, the gunners, because each battalion had a battery attached to it, the battery commander would be there, perhaps one of the sappers, any other special people. We met in the open and he said, "Now then, orders, here's the situation". He gave us a good situation report and the IO did a bit of that as well, telling everybody exactly where we were, what the Jap position was, and ours, and everything, which we'd not had at all before that. The form of it is, first of all, Information: who we all were, and roughly what was happening, and what we were going to do. Then Situation: which means what was known about the enemy, more about our own troops and the whole position. Then Execution: when you got the orders. So that put us really in the picture. He said, "Now the 4th Brigade, less the Lancashire Fusiliers, who are detached to 5th Brigade, so we're only a two battalion brigade, with Brigade TAC Headquarters we're going to do a right hook and try and come in behind the Japs, get on to the road that led from Kohima to Imphal, cut the road, shoot them up the arse!" It was as simple as that. *Lieutenant Sam Hornor, Signal Officer, HQ Coy, 2nd Norfolks*

This was a uniquely Robert Scott gloss on Grover's plan! The Brigade

Intelligence Officer could confirm that this plan was based on only a limited appreciation of the Japanese dispositions.

We knew it was the Japanese 31 Division. There were three regiments in this division: 58, which was very, very good indeed; 138 and 124, they were not quite as good or experienced in battle. A regiment is the same as an English brigade – it's three battalions. They made it so simple for one, their identity discs bore the number of their regiment, so even I could read from their identity discs that they belonged to 58 Regiment or 138 or 124 – in fact anybody could read it, Japanese numerals are not very difficult. There was a missing regiment – 124 – that we hadn't traced – we didn't know where the hell it had got to. We knew they were on GPT Ridge, Aradura was the mystery – we thought that Aradura didn't appear to be occupied. This was presumably confirmed by our air reconnaissance, although in that country air reconnaissance didn't tell you as much as you hoped. In fact being wise after the event we know that elements of 124 – the missing regiment – were there! *Captain John Howard, Intelligence Officer, HQ,4th Brigade*

The last minute preparations were chaotic and in the morass of last minute instructions Scott managed to pick a fight with Grover over the vexed issue of tin hats.

Then there was a funny little thing about hats on, hats off! Which is a great joke. Robert Scott said, "Bush hats will be worn!" General Grover said, "Tin hats will be worn!" Then there was a row between Robert and his Divisional commander. Robert didn't mind what he said, to whoever they were, he said, "Well that's a bloody silly order, Sir! They'd be much better if they had bush hats, much easier for the men". John Grover said, "Yes, I hear what you say, Robert, tin hats it is and stop arguing!" So we were hats in, hats out, of our kit-bags, one moment it was bush hats, then it was tin hats and we ended up with tin hats! *Lieutenant Sam Hornor, Signal Officer, HQ Coy, 2nd Norfolks*

The men were laden like packhorses as everything they needed had to be carried. There was no question of any kind of transport accompanying them.

We were issued with 100 rounds of ammunition in addition to what we already had. This we dangled round our necks in two bandoleers. Blankets were cut in half, we rolled half up and put it on the back of our pack. Every third man was given a shovel, every third man was given a pick and the other third were given two carriers of mortar bombs. *Sergeant Fred Hazell, D Coy, 2nd Norfolks*

The stronger men carried even more. 'Winkie' Fitt was now coming into his own as active service beckoned and he had been placed in command of No. 9 Platoon of B Company. His personal load would have tested a pack mule.

> Around my body, around my web belt, I had grenades all the way round. Other people that could, that were strong enough to do it, did the same. We also carried bandoleers of ammunition which we strung over our shoulders, or around our neck. I had about five or six bandoleers. About fifty rounds in a bandoleer I suppose. On top of that we had our ammunition pouches full. We were carrying anything and everything that we could in the way of ammunition and rations. We didn't expect the climb and the march to be quite as fierce as what it was. *Sergeant Bert Fitt, B Coy, 2nd Norfolks*

Hazell also made his own more personal preparations for 'Operation Strident'.

> This truck turned up so I nipped down there and I bought myself six cans of evaporated milk, half a pound of tea and about three pound of sugar. My pack was already stuffed tight but I managed to get this lot in because I didn't want to go on this three day trek without plenty of brewing up gear! *Sergeant Fred Hazell, D Coy, 2nd Norfolks*

It was known that there was a track of sorts leading to the Naga village of Khonoma. After that the country was considered to be almost impenetrable – certainly by a formation of armed troops. The maps were of limited use.

> They only arrived the night before. We had firstly half inch maps, that's the old map and then the maps which I carried myself up the hill was 1/25,000, which is about two-and-a-half inches to the mile. That was very good as far as it went but it was an air survey and the areas which are off the edge or coloured differently were an enlargement by the map making people of the old half inch – it was only the middle bits which were from a recent air survey. Of course the air survey bit was only what you could see from air photographs. But as far as they went they were very good. Although one always thought the map was wrong the map wasn't usually wrong – it was usually bad map reading. Very difficult of course in thick country. *Captain John Howard, Intelligence Officer, HQ, 4th Brigade*

Many officers however were less than impressed with the maps when they were distributed.

> We were looked at them and there was the map showing where we were going. It was absolutely white because it had never been surveyed, nobody had ever been there, the Nagas said they didn't go there because there was a lot of superstition about it – there were witches and that sort of thing. All there was, done from

aeroplanes was a few little nalas, watercourses and the rest of it was white – so it was a fat lot of use having a map! *Lieutenant Sam Hornor, Signal Officer, HQ Coy, 2nd Norfolks*

As the Iron Bridge area was under distant Japanese observation they set off on the march at about five o clock in the evening just as it started to get dark. (See map p160-161)

The path went up a steep valley between wooded slopes and climbed steadily, sometimes through trees and sometimes among paddy fields; often it became indistinguishable from field paths which led only to other areas of cultivation. *Captain John Howard, Intelligence Officer, HQ, 4th Brigade*[7]

The first stage, although through a cultivated area, still posed difficulties for the troops.

Very nasty, some of the time we were walking across paddy fields, not across the actual field itself but around its outskirts. They were built up like a ridge and it stank – have you ever smelt dead earth – it was horrible. *Bugler Bert May, HQ Coy, 2nd Norfolks*

Gradually they climbed up into the hills, with all the usual problems of marching through rough country with little or no light. Smoking was forbidden and every effort was taken to keep noise to a minimum.

God what a night that was! What a climb! What a climb! Very steep, wooded, a lot of undergrowth. There was a lot of paths but occasionally we had to cut our way through. I stepped on a moist tree root, lost my footing and fell flat on my back. My legs went in the air and I unfortunately caught the chap in front on both his legs, just above his knees and he was the biggest chap in the battalion. He came down on my stomach and God, he knocked every ounce of wind out of me. You couldn't hang about because it was pitch, blooming dark and if you lost the chap in front you could end up anywhere. *Sergeant Fred Hazell, D Coy 2nd Norfolks*

Eventually they arrived at Khonoma a village which had featured before in the proud annals of the British Army. For in 1879 it was here that Lieutenant Ridgeway of the 43rd Bengal Light Infantry had won a posthumous VC fighting the self same Nagas who would soon prove themselves indispensable to the Norfolks.

We finally arrived at this blessed village at about two o clock in the morning. Somebody from headquarters came up and said, "Put your platoon in there!" This was quite a big hut. We went in, pitch dark, I sat down on my backside, took my pack off and decided I was going to carry this evaporated milk not another inch! I drank four cans of it before I fell asleep. Long before I'd finished the whole platoon was snoring it's head off! I fell asleep myself. I woke up, the sun was shining through the chinks in the walls of this hut and I thought to myself, "God's strewth, I never posted a sentry!" I opened the door and there was a big Naga standing outside 'On Guard' with his spear. He looked round and he beamed at me, I patted him on the head. Then somebody appeared and said, "Have your breakfast, we're moving off at ten". 'Breakfast' was three biscuits and a brew up. *Sergeant Fred Hazell, D Coy 2nd Norfolks*

For the next three days the column moved mainly during the day, shielded from prying Japanese eyes by the thickness of the precipitous jungle ravines and ridges that surrounded them before tumbling down towards the Kohima road.

We moved off. I don't know quite how much we covered in the course of a day. Sometimes we only sort of scrambled down one ridge and scrambled up the next one. Some days we did a bit more. It was one long straight line of men on the move six foot apart, a massive great chain about quarter of a mile long. *Sergeant Fred Hazell, D Coy 2nd Norfolks*

Ahead of them went the men of the 143 Special Service Company.

McGeorge was commanding, and they were trained to go in front of the battalion and do a reconnaissance as we went round. Because we were on single tracks and we'd have been absolutely massacred, so he spread out and went round in front, rather like a broom going in front. *Second Lieutenant Dickie Davies, D Coy, 2nd Norfolks*

The Naga villagers had been formed into carrying parties and they took much of the heavier equipment for the struggling Norfolks.

About the second night, we were still doing a bit in the dark, I was conscious that there was another column moving along sort of ten foot away from me but in the same direction. In the dark I peered across there and it was Nagas, two or three hundred I should think. Men, women, young lads and even young girls carrying ammunition and water. There was young girls with a box of ammunition on their head tripping along quite gaily. We were staggering along underneath our packs! *Sergeant Fred Hazell, D Coy 2nd Norfolks*

The troops were incredibly impressed by the Naga porters whom they considered to have almost superhuman stamina and strength:

They grunted as they carried the thing. They had a sort of rhythm to them, "Grumm, brumm, Grumm, brumm", all the way up the hills. Funnily enough that stopped you getting out of breath, it was their expression of expelling their lungs. They'd been doing it for donkeys' years. For us it was something new carrying all that weight. They'd go on for ever and ever! They didn't like us stopping, they couldn't understand us stopping for ten minutes every hour. We were on our chin straps! *Sergeant Ben Macrae, Carrier Platoon, HQ Coy, 2nd Norfolks*

156

As they climbed higher the terrain got worse for the exigencies of war meant that the route was dictated to them by generals not geographers.

> We were moving across the country, not with it. The result being that we had to climb up one after another of these ridges, then slide down the other side and it was very, very exhausting. We were almost in single file, not quite perhaps, but a lot of the way through had to be cut and we had to have somebody ahead. We had these machetes and we cut our way to some extent. We even used ropes sometimes to get up very steep hills which were so slippery with the wet that you went forward one pace and back half a pace. It was very exhausting and very difficult but with the Nagas help we made it. But it was slow. Secrecy was very important, we didn't want the Japs to know we were coming in there behind the Jap lines – but there wasn't any lines if you know what I mean. We were well away from the actual battle going on in Kohima. *Lieutenant Sam Hornor, HQ Coy, 2nd Norfolks*

It was obvious that secrecy was paramount but the Medical Officer Captain John Mather illustrated why doctors and weapons were an unfortunate combination.

> I had a revolver but I'd no holster for it, I don't know why they didn't give me one, but I hadn't got one. It was sort of hanging loose on a cord. We were resting for a bit and suddenly there was a bang. I looked at my pistol and it was smoking! So I'd obviously fired it when I was sort of dozing and my hand was on it because it hadn't a cover. The sergeant came marching down because we were supposed to be silent. My batman said, "That was a Sten, Sergeant!" He said, "I know it was!" He said, "Well it was down there!" I never said a word! I got away with it! But I was lucky, I might have hit somebody or my own foot. Then I would have looked a 'B' fool wouldn't I? *Captain John Mather, Medical Officer, HQ Coy, 2nd Norfolks*

At intervals the rain poured down on the heaving column.

> I'm told that that part of the world has the heaviest rainfall in the world. I would never dispute that! It comes down in an absolute solid sheet. You think to yourself, "If it doesn't stop soon, beating against my poor skull, I'll go insane!" The whole area becomes a quagmire. Combined with the rain you got the humidity and you're sweating – the straps of your pack, your rifle sling and anything else you're carrying tends to chafe and rub. Your skin become sore all tender and raw. Your feet, however tough and hardened are saturated and become sore with constant rubbing, however well your boots are fitted. *Private Dick Fiddament, 2nd Norfolks*

After three days the column rested up in what was enticingly known as

'Death Valley'.

Death Valley, as it was soon called although no one died there, was a miserable place filled with huge trees covered in dripping moss. Sunlight rarely penetrated and rain was almost continuous. Here we lived on half 'light scale' rations for three days. Light scale rations consisted of milk, tea, sugar, bully beef and weevily biscuits.[8] *Captain John Howard, Intelligence Officer, HQ, 4th Brigade*

The men did not appreciate the fare that was provided.

The biscuits were about 4″ square and a ¹/₂″ thick. You would have thought it was mild steel plate that you were trying to get your teeth into. You had to break them with the end of your bayonet. *Sergeant Fred Hazell, D Coy, 2nd Norfolks*

As for the bully beef, Sergeant Macrae had had enough

I never liked it in the first place, I abhor it, it was something I endured. It's something that will go on my tombstone – he didn't like corned beef! *Sergeant Ben Macrae, Carrier Platoon, HQ Coy, 2nd Norfolks*

The troops were relieved to have the chance of proper rest but not overly impressed by their surroundings or the little 'friends' who welcomed them with open jaws.

It was a stinking hell of a hole. All the vegetation on the ground was dead, it stank to high heaven. I think that was why it got that name, not because there were any bodies lying around, but the actual stench of the place itself. Leeches, they used to get through on to any part of your body that was open. We tried to keep round the bottom of the trousers, round your sleeves and everything closed as much as you could. If we got leeches on us we never pulled them off, because the head stayed in the flesh and that made a very, very nasty ulcer. So you used to get a lighted cigarette, stick it on his tail and 'bonk' he used to pop off. You'd see blood, it would still be coming out. *Bugler Bert May, HQ Coy, 2nd Norfolks*

It was here under these unpropitious circumstances that Lieutenant Sam Hornor celebrated his 21st birthday.

Some of my chaps, almost to my embarrassment, thought that I ought to have birthday breakfast. So I had a very good breakfast of two biscuits, mashed up in my mess tin. Somebody got some brandy in a flask, tipped some in, somebody got some sugar, there was some powdered milk, that went in, it was all mushed up and then brewed up a bit over a little fire. The only way to light a fire was to burn ruppee notes, which we tended to carry in our pockets –

Sam Hornor

they were dry! So they fed me like that! *Lieutenant Sam Hornor, Signal Officer, HQ Coy, 2nd Norfolks*

They were all well aware that they were marching to what could be their deaths. John Howard and the Mortar Platoon commander, Lieutenant David Glasse, chatted together about their prospects.

David and I had spoken quietly about swimming and about his wife Louise in Hessle. We were not much worried. We were excited and although we realized that all would not survive this battle, we had no knowledge of the realities of war and felt little sadness at the prospect. I wondered what my reaction would be and how the loss of friends would strike me.[9] *Captain John Howard, Intelligence Officer, HQ, 4th Brigade*

Glasse was liked by many of his men.

David Glasse could come out and have a laugh and a joke with you, without losing any face. We used to say, "I wish he'd slow down!" He was always full of life wanting to 'go', egging everybody on. I used to reckon he was a scout master! He was a nice bloke, a grand chap really. *Sergeant Ben Macrae, Carrier Platoon, HQ Coy, 2nd Norfolks*

While the 4th Brigade rested they received orders to change their target from Aradura Spur to GPT Ridge. As intelligence officer John Howard was well placed to summarize the reasoning which lay behind this late change in plan.

Here we also received an order from Div HQ that instead of going behind the Japs on to the unoccupied Aradura Spur, we were to attack the flank of his known position on GPT Ridge, coming down on him from above. This entailed marching another two or three miles into country which he probably patrolled: it would be more difficult to achieve surprise in doing this than it would have been to establish ourselves on the Aradura and await his counter-attack which we knew we could defeat. Against moving to Aradura was the uncertainty of the Jap reaction. It might not force him out of his positions close in to Kohima. 5 Bde's move north of Kohima to the Merema track had attained its objectives but did not force the Jap out, and the result was a stalemate in the Naga village of Kohima just as it was on Garrison Hill. On Aradura we should have no line of communication, except our tortuous track through Khonoma, until GPT Ridge and Jail Hill were cleared. Our attack on GPT Ridge however would penetrate into the heart of the Jap position dominating Garrison Hill and we should then fairly easily make contact with our troops in the Jotsoma and Punjab Ridge area. An armoured column could also operate in our direction along the main road past Jail Hill. These, I think must have been the factors which

Long Trek of the Norfolks to GPT Ridge

Annotated map of Captain John Howard

Sachema

Mozema

FIRST NIGHT'S MARCH

Khonoma

6543

RE

Khurr N

SECOND DAYS MARCH

Dzuna N

NIGHT 26

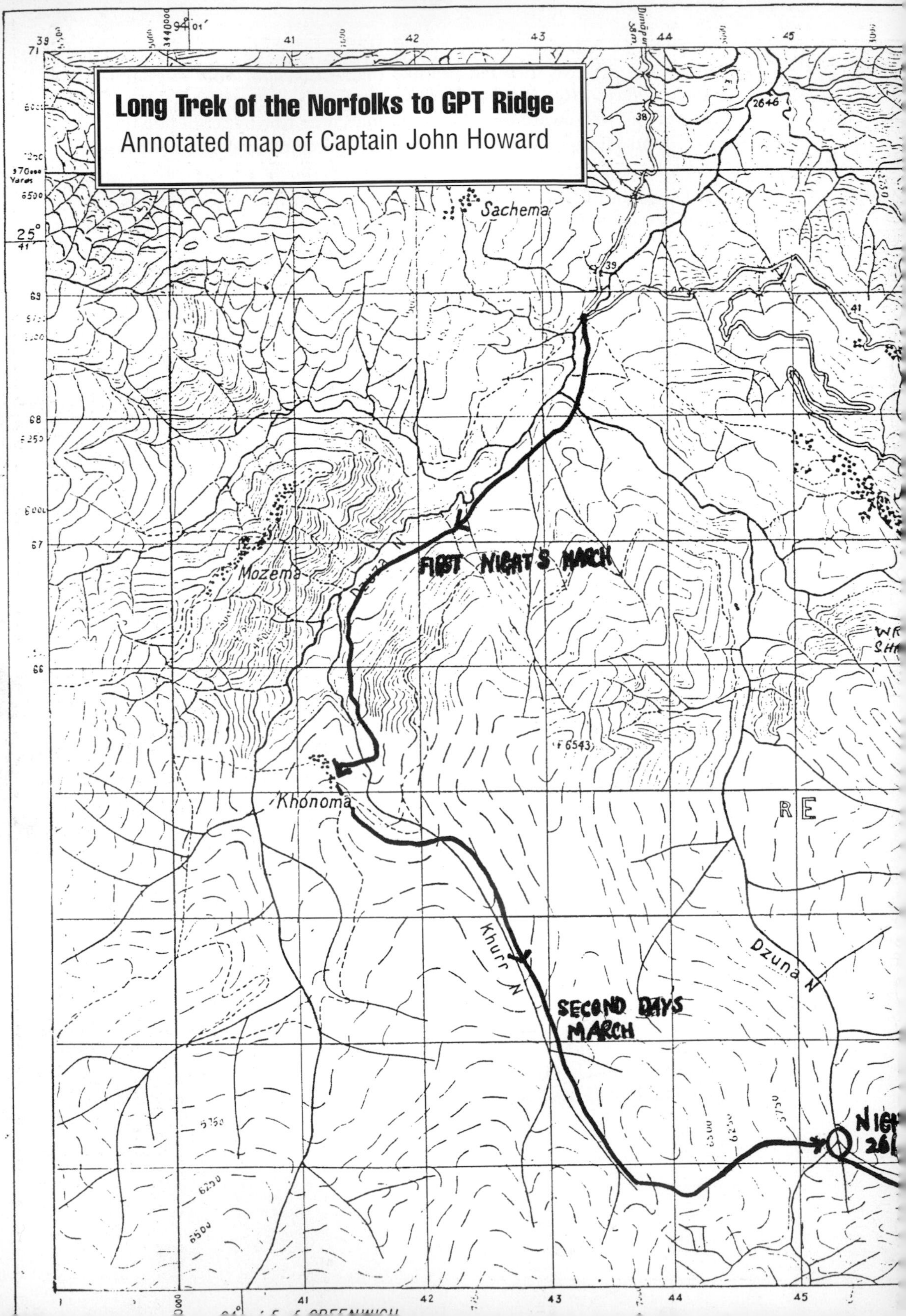

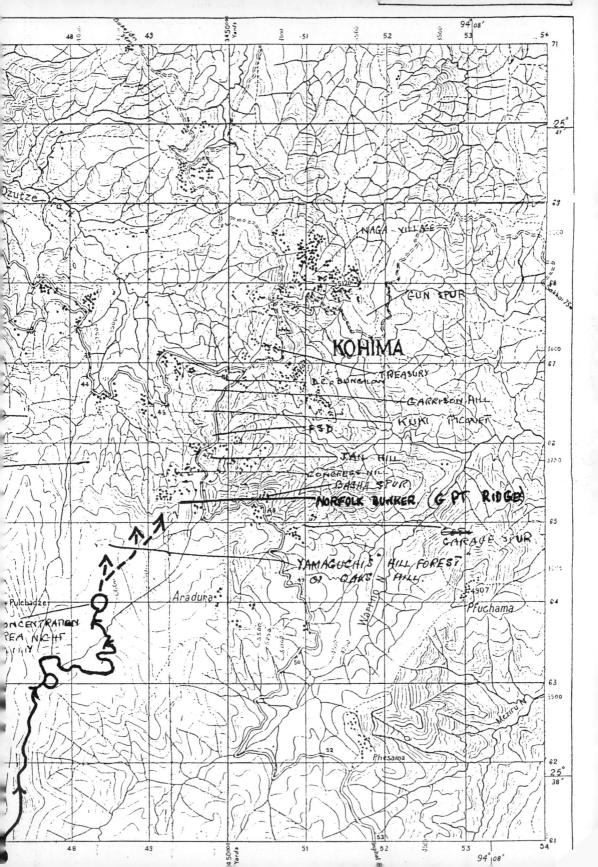

KOHIMA

NAGA VILLAGE

GUN SPUR

TREASURY

D.C. BUNGLOW

GARRISON HILL

KUKI PICWET

FSD

JAIL HILL

CONGRESS HILL

BASHA SPUR

NORFOLK BUNKER (G PT RIDGE)

GARAGE SPUR

YAMAGUCHI'S HILL FOREST OF OAKS HILL

Dzutze

Aradura

Pulebadzer

CONCENTRATION AREA NIGHT

Pfuchama

Phesama

A section of Japanese mountain artillery in action firing 75mm guns which had a range of 9,800 yards.   Taylor Library

caused General Grover to direct us to GPT Ridge instead of Aradura. Whether he was right ot not is impossible to tell.[10]
Captain John Howard, Intelligence Officer, HQ, 4th Brigade

One concern to Grover was the slow rate of progress, but the men could not possibly go any faster in the conditions. The whole distance they had to march from the road to GPT Ridge was only around seven miles on the map, but in the Assam jungle mere miles had little or no value as a unit of human measurement.

The physical hammering one takes is difficult to understand. The heat, the humidity, the altitude and the slope of almost every foot of ground, combine to knock hell out of the stoutest constitution. You gasp for air which doesn't seem to come, you drag your legs upwards till they seem reduced to the strength of matchsticks, you wipe the salt sweat out of your eyes. Then you feel your heart pounding so violently you think it must burst its cage; it sounds as loud as a drum, even above the swearing and cursing going on around you. So you stop, horrified, to be prodded by the man behind or cursed by an officer in front.

Eventually, long after everything tells you you should have died of heart failure, you reach what you imagine is the top of the hill only to find it is a false crest, and the path still lies upwards. And when you finally get to the top, there is a hellish climb down. You forget the Japs, you forget time, you forget hunger and thirst. All you can think of is the next halt.[11] *Lieutenant Sam Hornor, Signal Officer, HQ Coy, 2nd Norfolks*

In these circumstances the column could only progress at its own speed. While the brigade rested in Death Valley, Major Conder took a small patrol, selected from B Company, up the mountain which lay to the south. They were to ensure that no Japanese patrols were lurking in that direction ready to fall on the right flank of the column.

We went out to the highest peak in the area covering a village. We were looking down on to it and Major Conder went back to the battalion. I remained there all night with a standing patrol where you cover a position observing what's going on. We were straddling a path which led up from the village, through to another village, most probably to the left of us. Round about midnight there was movement on the track and this chap came along. We didn't know who he was and he came right close to where I was with my HQ. I got him, put my hand over his mouth, held a knife into his back and told him to keep quiet, which he did. The poor fellow was scared stiff and he must have thought we were going to kill him. He was a Naga but we daren't let him go, because we didn't know whether he would go and tell the Japanese where we were or what we were doing. So I had to hold him all night. I took him into our headquarters where he couldn't be seen and told him if he kept quiet he would not get hurt. Lucky enough he could understand what we meant, he laid down and went to sleep, he didn't bother. The next morning when it was daylight we let the man go on his way, because we were moving off from that position, so we didn't mind. I took my patrol back to rejoin my company. *Sergeant Bert Fitt, B Coy, 2nd Norfolks*

On 1 May, after a further horrendous climb up precipitous slopes which required the engineers to cut out steps and erect rope lines for the men to haul themselves up, the column ascended on to the ridge above Aradura and GPT Ridge.

By nightfall we had scrambled about a mile to the north along the crest and were established on the wooded peaks above Aradura... The ridge top was a strange contrast to the valley. Sometimes the clouds were below us and we were bathed in brilliant sunshine; at other times the clouds were all around us. The view was nearly always restricted by clouds below or clouds close about us. We looked down into the forest for a hundred feet on either side of us and then the steeply falling hill was hidden in

JAPVO PEAK
9890 feet

SOUTH END OF
PULEBADZE RIDGE

ARADURA
SPUR

NORFOLK
RIDGE

RIFLE
RANGE

GPT RIDGE

ROAD TO
IMPHAL

PIMPLE

CONGRESS
HILL

JAIL HILL

DIS HILL

FSD HILL

K

DISTRICT COMMISSIONER
BUNGALOW AND TENNIS
COURT

PULEBADZE RIDGE
77532 feet

JOTSOMA TRACK

GARRISON HILL

The Norfolks were up against one of the most dedicated and fanatical fighting machines that the 20th Century had produced to that date.
Taylor Library

the swirling white blanket. Sudden showers of rain were frequent but such water as fell ran swiftly away, as from a roof. We were able to look across to Garrison Hill and Naga Village but it was too distant a view to be of much practical use. We saw Jail Hill and the extreme north eastern tip of GPT Ridge our objective, but the rest of it and all the approaches to it were hidden and indistinguishable in the thick jungle.[12] *Captain John Howard, Intelligence Officer, HQ, 4th Brigade*

On the afternoon of 2 May they descended from the ridge into the upper reaches of the Aradura Valley, crossed it and climbed again to the spur above GPT Ridge.

We settled down for the night. We were all feeling fairly relieved that: A) The march had finished and B) We'd got there without being discovered. We had the advantages of surprise on our side. So it was a bit of a bitter pill when at about two o'clock in the morning all hell let loose behind us. It was only then that I was told that the Royal Scots were following a day behind us in reserve. Unfortunately a Jap patrol had bumped into them, they'd seen the Nagas that had been carrying our baggage and followed them. Of course the Nagas took the same route back as the Royal Scots were coming forward, so they passed each other and the Japs then walked straight into the Royal Scots who opened up on them with everything they'd got. Of course we heard, so the Japs heard it and then they knew there was someone behind their lines. *Sergeant Fred Hazell, D Coy 2nd Norfolks*

At this point the column thought they were on Oaks Hill and reported this to Divisional Headquarters who were baffled as they had numerous reports from patrols that Oaks Hill was in the hands of the Japanese. This mistake was not really surprising given the difficulties in navigating through extremely rough terrain with inadequate maps. On 3 May Brigadier William Goschen took out a 22 man reconnaissance patrol to try and determine exactly where they were and to allow the proper planning of the forthcoming assault on GPT Ridge next day. No less than eight of the Norfolks accompanied the party as they had been selected to lead the attack.

We could see absolutely bugger all. I suppose we were a couple of miles from the road and immediately below one was heavy jungle. I know it was clear down by the road but they were all reverse convex slopes and you couldn't see what was beyond the slope. It was too far away. I saw two chaps walking along the road but even with binoculars you couldn't tell whether they were soldiers, Japs or Nagas – they might have been anybody. *Captain John Howard, Intelligence Officer, HQ, 4th Brigade*

After much furtive searching the Brigadier managed to find a spot

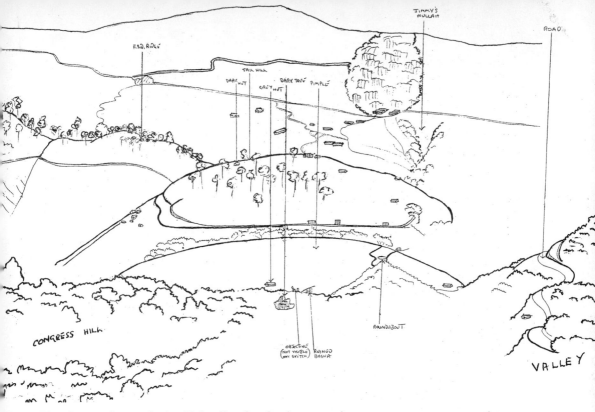

Sketch map drawn during Brigadier Goschen's reconnaissance.

where he could just see the corrugated iron roof of a building which it was considered might be at the bottom end of GPT Ridge. They took a compass bearing and it was on this flimsy basis that the Brigadier made his plans.

No one had seen the ground beyond the point of our reconnaissance, but we believed we were about five hundred yards from the edge of the trees and that beyond lay the barren northeast end of GPT Ridge. In fact, we were much higher up the hill and some twelve hundred yards from the edge of the jungle. About the enemy, we knew he had positions on the barren end of GPT Ridge, that he patrolled between there and us, that he had further positions on Jail Hill and that the bridge at milestone 47 was a hive of activity. We also knew of the Japs that had attacked the Royal Scots on the Japvo-Pulebadze Ridge. It appeared that we still had the advantage of surprise, for the Jap gave no indication that he knew of our presence in strength on his flank.[13] *Captain John Howard, Intelligence Officer, HQ, 4th Brigade*

This was extremely minimal information on which to base plans for an attack. Yet a balance had to be struck between ignorance and more

167

PIMPLE

JAIL HILL

DIS HILL

Jail Hill in the bottom left hand corner and the lower slopes of GPT Ridge.

active patrolling which may have elicited more information, but was likely to prejudice surprise.

A plan based on such scanty information had of necessity to be fluid. Two platoons of the Special Service Company were placed under Robert Scott's command, in order to patrol ahead of the Norfolk while they approached their start line which was to be one hundred yards above the edge of the trees. During this approach, 99th Field Regiment and other regiments of guns, were to register on the barren portion of GPT Ridge and to fire diversionary concentrations on to Jail Hill and the ring contour hillock at the end of GPT on the opposite side of the road to Jail Hill. When the Norfolks were ready to leave the start line they were to call for a concentration of all guns on to their objective.[14] *Captain John Howard, Intelligence Officer, HQ, 4th Brigade*

Fundamentally it was an advance to contact by the Norfolks. When they reached the edge of the jungle on GPT Ridge they were to inform Divisional Headquarters who would unleash an artillery barrage prior to the final assault on the lower ridge. Meanwhile the Royal Scots would initially guard their rear and then act as brigade reserve to be used in an exploitation attack on the hillock at the end of GPT Ridge if the Norfolks succeeded. Unfortunately these plans were disrupted before they had even been given out.

While the Brigadier was giving these orders, a patrol led by Roger Bostock reported that there was a Japanese position between us and the proposed start line. Our faces fell. The Brigadier questioned Roger as to whether he was certain that it was a defended locality and not just a patrol. Roger was quite certain. The Brigadier scratched the back of his neck, chewed his straggling moustache and made up his mind quickly. His plan would not be altered in its main outline. If the Japanese were still there in the morning, the position, which appeared to be isolated, would be contained and by-passed.[15] *Captain John Howard, Intelligence Officer, HQ, 4th Brigade*

Thus briefed Scott called his battalion 'O' Group together.

The light was failing fast so he said, "Get your pencils out, I'm going to give you the fire plan first, its important you should have it written down while you can see to write". He did that and I wrote down the fire plan in my notebook. By then it was dark. He said, "Orders, memorize the lot, they're going to be simple!" *Lieutenant Sam Hornor, HQ Coy, 2nd Norfolks*

The 4th Platoon of the dismounted Carrier Company was to move forward before dawn to be in position at the foot of Oaks Hill by 05.30. They were to cover the main body of the battalion as it moved down in the order: A Company under Major Swainson; D Company under

Japanese troops bringing up ammunition over difficult terrain.   Taylor Library

Major Hatch; the battalion TAC HQ; the medics; HQ Company under Major Boldero; C Coy under Major Murray-Brown; and finally B Company in reserve under Major Twidle.

Sergeant Macrae of the 4th Platoon was ordered to take out a night patrol with the twin aims of locating the Japanese positions and familiarizing himself with the route.

I took the last patrol out that night and I had to find out where the Japs were down there because during the day this knocking, banging was coming closer. I asked, "Who's in front?" to the Special Service Platoon. Their Sergeant said, "Anyone in front of us, you meet will be Japs!" I went down the hill and I think there'd been a skirmish with the SS the night before because I discovered one of the SS chaps down there dead and the Japanese had taken his boots. So I knew that the Japs had been up to there. I took my three blokes all the way down, right up to the nala. It was a dry nala, all big stones, not one of these things like sand that you could have crept across, you'd have made a devil of a noise. I got on another track that was running alongside it. At the end of this track, 20 or 30 yards away, there was the Japanese positions and 100/1 they'd got automatic guns trained all the way around us. I got right up close and you could hear voices and movement. We'd found out where they were and that they were in there in some strength. My report went through the channels straight the way

170

back to Bob Scott at battalion headquarters. *Sergeant Ben Macrae, Carrier Platoon, HQ Coy, 2nd Norfolks*

Scott was determined that, before they set off on the following day, his men should have something hot inside them.

The Doctor had dug a hole for the Regimental Aid Post. Robert Scott had strict orders from brigade that there were to be no fires lit whatsoever. He disobeyed the order, told the Doctor, "Look here get a fire going in the bottom of that ruddy hole of yours and I want every man to have some hot tea, I think it's very important for morale!" There was little or no smoke, any smoke that filtered up, there was somebody to swoosh it away. Brigadier Goschen then discovered that this was going on and practically placed Robert Scott under arrest – but not quite! Robert talked his way out of it and said, "It's essential for the men to have poultices on their legs because they're getting bad and it'll get worse – we've got to look after the men's' health!" *Lieutenant Sam Hornor, Signal Officer, HQ Coy, 2nd Norfolks*

Not all the men got their cup of tea, but those that did appreciated the risk taken by Scott with his career and their lives. To them it was worth it!

I received some tea in my mess tin – hot tea! You don't know what a cup of tea means to you after you've been three or four days marching without having one. A cup of tea does marvels! *Bugler Bert May, HQ Coy, 2nd Norfolks*

They were facing the culmination of all their years of training, they were to go into action in just a few hours. Most men, not surprisingly, were still nervous despite their refreshing 'cuppa'.

Everybody's frightened. If he says he's not, then he's either a liar, or a bloody madman. Because nobody wants to die, but nobody. I certainly didn't. But you're all pals together, there's a job to do and you get on with it the best way you can. *Private Dick Fiddament, 2nd Norfolks*

Other men gained added strength as they concentrated on their responsibility to the men that served under them.

I was happy as a platoon commander. I was prepared for a good scrap, if there was one coming along and I didn't fear anything or anybody. I was keen to learn and I was also keen to try and protect the men that were under my command. I wanted to go into battle with thirty men and come out with thirty men. That was my idea and as far as the leadership was concerned, I never asked any troops under me to do what I couldn't or wouldn't do myself. I wasn't frightened. About a couple of minutes before the attack, you'd get a sick feeling in the stomach. But immediately you moved, that sick feeling goes away altogether as far as I was concerned. I mean everybody, I don't care who he is, is nervous to a certain extent until the actual battle starts. But when the battle starts then you've got one thing in your mind, it's either you or the enemy, but somebody is going to get killed. At the back of your mind it's the enemy that's going to get killed, not you, or your men as far as that goes. *Sergeant Bert Fitt, B Coy, 2nd Norfolks*

Fitt and his platoon taken in the Kohima area. Fitt is third from the right at the front, marked by an arrow. The fate of these men was in his hands.

CHAPTER TEN

Capture of GPT Ridge

Just before dawn on 4 April the 4th Platoon moved down the hill following in the footsteps of Corporal Macrae and his patrol the previous night.

It was half light when I first went down the hill. I knew where they were and I had to try and get as close as I could to find out could I deal with them or what! I observed a good six Japanese floating around – one leaning against a tree smoking, another two digging a pit right by the nala. I think they must have seen or heard all the A Company coming up behind me because suddenly they all darted into their foxholes and bunkers. I was told to go in and deal with them, but I saw there was far too many and I couldn't get across that nala in time to do anything. We'd have been wiped out before we even got there. I went back and saw Russell, the Intelligence Sergeant, "Who've you seen Benny?", he said. I told him, "I've only seen six but there's a lot more Japs behind digging in up the hill". It rose quite sharply the other side of the nala and I knew they were digging in there. By then we'd fired on them, I think we got a couple and one of my chaps had been wounded. *Sergeant Ben Macrae, Carrier Platoon, HQ Coy, 2nd Norfolks*

As A Coy arrived they covered the Japanese bunker whilst the rest of the battalion moved round to the right to avoid the obstacle. D Company now took over the lead role. They moved through the thick jungle on a two section front with the men only a couple of yards apart tearing their way through a mixture of thorn trees, bramble, bamboo and miscellaneous undergrowth.

Captain Fulton, the second in command of D Company, sat down on a log with me, just sort of chatting for a moment. He said, "Well, Sam, better get off and earn my MC!" Off he rushed and ten seconds later he was shot through the head by a sniper. That's the way it went. *Lieutenant Sam Hornor, Signal Officer, HQ Coy, 2nd Norfolks*

Despite their loss the company continued forward, moving down the ridge, but not along the crest which was held by the Japanese.

We started advancing slowly through the trees. We hadn't gone 50 yards before we came under fire. The Japs had moved towards us and positioned themselves up in the trees, strapped up in the trees, so that when you fired they didn't fall out when they got hit. We advanced through them so that we were being shot at from

173

both the front and the back. A shot whistled past my head and I thought to myself, "Jesus!" I ran forward to a tree and lay down beside it, poked my rifle forward and poked my head round the tree. Obviously whoever it was was waiting for me to do just that because another shot rang out and it hit the tree. The bark opened up and stuck in my cheeks all down there. I thought I'd been hit and I sort of rolled back and I felt it – of course that only pushed the splinter into my face all the more. There was no blood, I thought, "That's funny!" I picked all these little pieces out. I thought I was off back to Calcutta at that stage. *Sergeant Fred Hazell, D Coy, 2nd Norfolks*

The iron disciplined fire control that the Norfolks had refined in so many exercises was a severe disadvantage in the reality of jungle warfare. The Japanese concealed themselves skilfully to ensure that they opened up first to devastating effect in any fire fight.

This is one of the reasons we lost as many men as we did. Had we gone forward spraying we would probably have done better. But our instructions always were, "Don't fire till you see the whites of their eyes". Bearing in mind that this ammunition had been carried for nine days round these confounded hills you didn't want to go spraying it about! By and large this discipline was maintained. *Sergeant Fred Hazell, D Coy, 2nd Norfolks*

Major Hatch reported the situation back to Scott at the TAC HQ which was following immediately behind D Company. He was ordered to bear left and up the side of the ridge to get as high as possible.

We got stuck, everybody stopped and nothing seemed to happen. It was very interesting because we'd been told time and time again in training, "Don't shoot your rifle unless you've got a target, it's no good just blazing off, ammunition is precious, don't waste it – always go for a target". So we got stuck, we were obeying all our training orders and we weren't shooting at all, we couldn't see anything. Robert Scott realized at once what was happening and just shouted in all directions, "Start blasting them and advance. Shoot up in the trees, get shooting!" Once he'd given the order away we went! *Lieutenant Sam Hornor, Signal Officer, HQ Coy, 2nd Norfolks*

The pace of the advance increased as the men sprayed the undergrowth and trees all around them, throwing grenades with enthusiasm. As the jungle began to open out in front of them Hazell had a nerve wrenching escape.

When we got out of the long grass I said to the lads, "Get down on your hands and knees and crawl!" We came out into the open. There was this slope going up, fairly open and a grenade landed, believe it or not, between my hands, it rolled out between my knees and feet, under the chap behind me. I yelled out and flattened myself out, as everybody else did and the grenade went off. I thought to myself, "Oh my godfathers!" I turned round expecting to see this chap in shreds. Instead of which he was sitting back on his haunches. He looked at me and he blinked. I said, "Are you all right?" He said, "Yeah!" He opened his shirt and the grenade had disintegrated into a powder. It looked like there were hundreds of blackheads on his chest which you could squeeze all out. He spat out a bit of blood here and there but he seemed to be perfectly all right and he carried on. I believe quite a lot of the Jap grenades were like that, they were very inferior and instead of breaking up into nasty pieces of metal they just completely disintegrated. *Sergeant Fred Hazell, D Coy, 2nd Norfolks*

D Company ran into the clearing to be confronted by a Japanese bunker which they charged.

When we got to the top of the ridge it was almost like World War One. There were four, five or six Japs, I imagine they must have run out of ammunition, but they suddenly leapt out of their holes and raced at us with their bayonets. They held them up in the air. Of course they didn't get very far because the lads' machine guns just went 'BZZZZTTT' like that. They threw their rifles at us but it was fairly simple to side-step them. They were about 12 yards away when they finally hurled them at us as they dropped. *Sergeant Fred Hazell, D Coy, 2nd Norfolks*

The reserve company was moved up ready for the next phase of the attack from the edge of the jungle down across the open area of GPT Ridge. They passed the mortally wounded Captain Fulton.

We went from the forming up place, got on to the start line. I remember seeing some of them laying, in particular, poor old Micky Fulton, Captain Fulton, he had been hit through the top of his head and the scalp was laying open. You could see his brain actually moving and he had a pleading look in his eye, more or less asking you with appearance to put a bullet through him and finish him off. Well you couldn't do that,

Michael Fulton

you wouldn't do it anyway. But it was obvious that he hadn't long to go. *Sergeant Bert Fitt, B Coy, 2nd Norfolks*

The men moved past as Fulton's last moments slipped away.

I saw Fulton lying on the path with a bullet through his head. He was clawing at his watch as if he had to see what the time was, but I think it was just a nervous reaction, poor chap. *Bugler Bert May, HQ Coy, 2nd Norfolks*

As the forward companies fought their way forward the medics followed picking up the pieces.

I kept up with the troops, I was running part of the way and so were my chaps. They and I dealt with anybody who was injured. Gave them the treatment and left them behind for other people to take back. Morphine that's the main thing. We had some special tubes about two inches long, they were like toothpaste tubes. There was a needle on it which you could break off, turn round and put on so that when you squeezed the tube the morphine solution came out of the needle. You pushed the needle in and of course they got the morphine. You had a little label to stick on them. Severe pain causes shock and if you relieve the pain you tend to relieve the shock. If the wound was very filthy you'd clean it up with an antiseptic – flavine. If there was a lot of bleeding you had to get a pack on and bind it up. A strip of bandage with a wad of cotton wool attached to it. Every chap had one tucked into his dressing pocket and you could take that off, put it on and bind it up. Then it would depend on the size of the wound. If it was only small we'd perhaps use his dressing, but if it was any size we'd got some bigger ones – wrap them round, that protected it and kept the dirt out. If there were enough stretcher bearers handy they could perhaps move him, or just leave him and let other people catch up. *Captain John Mather, Medical Officer, HQ Coy, 2nd Norfolks*

Hornor had a particularly testing role as signal officer.

I was to stick with the CO, stick with TAC HQ, with the signal corporal and his wireless set, which was of critical importance. That was our communication with the whole battalion. I had to stick with him all the time – it was as simple as that. Keep a watch on everything that was going on and be prepared to pass messages. If I got a message from one of the companies I'd tell the CO immediately. *Lieutenant Sam Hornor, Signal Officer, HQ Coy, 2nd Norfolks*

He was therefore mortified when a valve failed in the radio.

There was a pause and the wireless set went, 'Phutt!' So I said to Colk, "Right on the ground we get, we've got to get this ruddy thing working again!" They were valve radios and the platoon was very well trained in changing valves by sequence, testing all the time. They knew what they felt like and we just solemnly started doing it. I think it took seven or eight minutes, it seemed to take an age, with growling from Robert Scott behind, "Bloody wireless sets, bloody signallers!" But that was normal, you didn't pay any attention to that. We just worked away at it and then, thank goodness, between us we got it right and away she went! *Lieutenant Sam Hornor, Signal Officer, HQ Coy, 2nd Norfolks*

D Company had done sterling work as the assault company and had cleared GPT Ridge up to the fringe of the jungle by 12.30. The battalion closed up on the start line in preparation for the next stage of the attack on the lower ridge. It was to be undertaken by platoons drawn from A and B Company. 'Winkie' Fitt was getting impatient.

We should have had artillery support. That was all laid on to blast GPT Ridge before we attacked it. But things got rather desperate as we laid on the start line for my company. We were getting shot up and hadn't got a chance. *Sergeant Bert Fitt, B Coy, 2nd Norfolks*

Men of action took control along the Norfolks' front line.

I lost my Bren gunner, a chap named Grogan. I grabbed the Bren and I had a rifle slung on my shoulder. I said "Right", and I called out to Davis who was commanding the left hand platoon. I told him I had had enough laying here and not fighting. I was going forward. Lieutenant Reeve in the centre, he had to come with us. *Sergeant Bert Fitt, B Coy, 2nd Norfolks*

While Fitt fretted, Colonel Scott decided that if he was to maintain any kind of momentum in the attack and capitalize on D Company's achievement they could not afford any more time waiting.

According to the orders, there should have been a pause. The 99th Field Regiment was all ready for the word, " Fire!" to put down heavy fire on our objective. Robert Scott decided, absolutely rightly, that the momentum was going and he kept it going. The Battery Commander said, "What about the guns?" "No! No! Forget it, we'll just get straight on through". He went right on as far as it was possible to get. *Lieutenant Sam Hornor, Signal Officer, HQ Coy, 2nd Norfolks*

Scott was itching to be at the sharp end of the battle. Finally it all got too much for him.

He just disappeared, he ran off, it was left to the initiative of the company commanders, they knew what they had got to do. They knew themselves when they'd got to stop – they couldn't get any further. He ran off with A Company who were then the spearhead and practically led the assault. *Lieutenant Sam Hornor, Signal Officer, HQ Coy, 2nd Norfolks*

Scott's behaviour was not in any way conventional.

> He was just bloody ridiculous. He behaved as a Colonel shouldn't behave. He was always with the leading sections if possible. He was way up forward during the advance to contact down GPT Ridge. Fortunately Henry Conder, who was a very able soldier, was there at battalion headquarters and managed to keep things going smoothly and orderly, even though Robert was behaving as a platoon commander. *Captain John Howard, Intelligence Officer, HQ, 4th Brigade*

Re-examined more objectively, perhaps Scott appeared to have divined an essential truth of jungle warfare.

> In this jungle fighting you can't, as an officer, a platoon commander, or company commander, you can't give orders to people ahead, where they're to go, what they're to do, because you can't see – the officers have got to lead from the front. That is a characteristic of jungle warfare. That's what Robert Scott was doing – he was leading the attack from the front where he could see what was going on. You couldn't give orders to someone in front if you couldn't see. *Lieutenant Sam Hornor, Signal Officer, HQ Coy, 2nd Norfolks*

The 'raging' Colonel joined in the attack which was launched at around 14.35.

> Bob Scott lined us up with Bren guns, we'd got a sling over your shoulder, taking the weight, with a man behind us with extra ammunition. Bob Scott at that time was ill with malaria and all he had was a pistol and his cud stick. His famous words were, "Right-ho boys, lets go!" That was it, the instructions were to fire at everything, spraying some down, some up and forward of course, because there was a bunker there. Up to that time I had not seen a Japanese at all. But hidden in this semi-clearing, low bushes, that sort of thing, several got up and started running away. They didn't run far because the amount of fire power was terrific, about 12 Bren guns. I heard Bert Davis was hit because he shouted, "Robbo, take over, it's yours!" The bunker was taken, I never went in, there were just grenades thrown in and somebody went in to make sure it was clear and that was it. *Sergeant William Robinson, A Coy, 2nd Norfolks*

Sergeant Fitt was leading the right hand platoon of the attack.

> We attacked, we went straight in with the bayonet, with what we'd got and we took the position. I used this Bren gun for the remainder of that attack, running with it using it from the hip. The Japanese positions were facing outwards. So they had to come out into the open if they wanted to fight us and that suited us. We wanted them in the open so that we could see what was going on.

Right: *A captured Japanese bunker in the Kohima ar*
IWM IND3484

178

Japanese 70 mm gun with mechanism in the lowest firing position.
Taylor Library

We tore down GPT Ridge as fast as we could go. We were coming into the open. You'd got some places that were thick, other places were more open and then there was more of a track going down. About half way down, leading my right hand platoon, I saw what looked like to me like a piece of flat ground and I thought perhaps that was a bunker, facing the opposite way. I jumped on to this parapet and when I looked down I was looking down the muzzle of a mountain field gun. I threw a grenade in because I knew there was people still there. Three got out and my runner, a chap named Swinscoe, he came up on his shoulder with his rifle and he shot the first one that was running away from us over the valley. He twizzled him like a rabbit – a marvellous shot – he got him all right. We'd then got two prisoners. *Sergeant Bert Fitt, B Coy, 2nd Norfolks*
The 70 mm gun captured by Fitt and his men stands guard today at the entrance of the Royal Norfolk Regiment Museum at Castle Hill in Norwich. The prisoners unfortunately met a more sudden fate.

I left these two prisoners with one man, a soldier you could trust, and told him to bring them along, I said search them before you bring them. Colonel Scott came up. I told him we'd got these prisoners and he said "Where are they?" I told him that they were being brought along by one of the chaps and he said "Good!" Well up came this fellow, no prisoners so I asked him where they were.

The 70 mm gun captured by Fitt and his men.

He said, "Back there, up the track". I said, "What do you mean? They're going to be gone!" He said, "Never, they won't go anywhere! Remember my brother got bayoneted in a hospital bed. When I searched them I took these badges off them. These are the Territorial Army badges what they had". I said "That's right, yes they are". He said "Well, I bayoneted them, both of them, I killed them". So I had to go and tell the CO. When I told him, that we hadn't got the prisoners, he flew at me and said, "Bring the person who let them escape to me!" I said "They didn't escape, they took these badges off them – they are officers' badges of the 4th, 5th, or 6th Battalion". He said, "Yes, so what?" I said, "Well, his brother was bayoneted in bed in hospital – he bayoneted them and got his own back". Colonel Scott said, "That's saved me cutting their bloody throats!" *Sergeant Bert Fitt, B Coy, 2nd Norfolks*

The objective was gained and consolidation was imperative in case of Japanese counter-attacks.

Everybody got as far as they could, so the word went round, "Dig in!" We dug in there and it was the top of GPT ridge. Robert got on the wireless and said, "Objective captured!" There was a code word for it I think. Divisional headquarters started coming through to the Brigadier saying, "What about the fire plan – you haven't had the fire plan yet!" He just said, "Well Robert wouldn't have it, he just didn't want it and they went straight on through to the objective without it!" Then Robert got on and sent a message to the Divisional Commander, "If you don't believe me, come and bloody well look!" *Lieutenant Sam Hornor, Signal Officer, HQ Coy, 2nd Norfolks*

As can be imagined Scott's relaxed approach grated a little at brigade and divisional headquarters.

The Brigadier was fuming and fretting, division were fuming and fretting saying, "Don't you want the artillery? Don't you want the artillery?" We said, "No, we're not ready yet!" They said, "You ought to have been!" Then somewhere about mid-afternoon the Norfolks did condescend to get on the radio to say that, "We've captured our objective!" "What with no artillery?" "Yes, with no artillery!" *Captain John Howard, Intelligence Officer, HQ, 4th Brigade*

On the left of the attack they slightly over-ran the objective and came under heavy machine-gun fire from a complex series of bunker positions, soon to be known as 'Norfolk Bunker', about 40 yards away on their left front further down GPT Ridge towards the Kohima road. They could go no further and so the priority became consolidation of the gains they had made all along GPT Ridge.

Someone shouted out, "We've arrived – dig in – prepare yourselves for a counter-attack. Fortunately at that spot there were plenty of old Japanese holes. At that time I had 12-14 men left, the others were wounded mainly. I dropped a couple of men in this hole, a couple of men there, a couple of men there. All the time you were being fired at. We didn't appreciate at that stage when we stopped that there was this confounded bunker about 70 yards in front of us, with umpteen machine guns inside it. At that moment Major Hatch appeared and he said, "Come with me, I want to sort the company positions out for the night". With that he strode through the positions I'd got my lads in and started going down towards this bunker which I don't think he was aware of. Of course I had to follow him. We were standing there in the open

Dennis Hatch

area with this bunker down here on our left and he was saying, "That would be a good place to have a Bren gunner – there!". All the time bullets were whistling past our heads and I was thinking to myself, "Crikey! How on earth are we going to get men to dig in there?" He said to me, "We're being fired at, lets make ourselves less conspicuous". He dropped down on his hands and knees. I dropped down with him, I was nearest to the bunker and my head was level with his waist. A shot rang out and I thought it had taken my nose off. Godfathers, it was bloody painful! I went, "OOOOOHHH! They've got my bloody nose!" I put my hand up there and my nose was still there! "No, they haven't! Missed me!" What had happened was I think it had passed under my nose – I had a blister come up. The Major said, "It missed you, but I think it's hit me". I looked and it had got him in the leg, in an artery unfortunately. I tried to put a tourniquet on but I had nothing really to do the job properly with. I dragged him back under cover, over the ridge and handed him over to the medics. I was very upset in the morning when they told me he had died in the night. *Sergeant Fred Hazell, D Coy, 2nd Norfolks*

The officers and NCOs organized their men into a rough battalion perimeter. Unfortunately there were few of them left unwounded.

Twidle got hit through the stomach and that knocked him out altogether. He had to hand over to Randle. Captain Randle was a very quiet, reserved man, nobody knew what his fighting qualities were. Randle was hit in the leg – more of a walking wounded. If you got hit out there we were so low in numbers, you couldn't afford to stop for a minor injury. You had to carry on fighting and that was that. The CO had been hit, a scalp wound, it wasn't too serious. With him he was such a hard nut, that you'd got to knock his head off if you wanted to call it serious with him. We were very, very thin on the ground then, for leaders. *Sergeant Bert Fitt, B Coy, 2nd Norfolks*

Again the endless training paid dividends for the platoon sergeants had considerable tactical acumen and were well able to deploy their men in accordance with basic military principles.

We then went round, because I had already consolidated my platoon in such a position that I was covering the right flank of the battalion. I inter-laced my light machine guns, I had three, so I could cover, with the right hand gun, right along the front of my company area. With the left hand gun I could do the same. So if anything happened all you've got to do is press the trigger of the guns and they'd have to walk through a stream of bullets. We went right down to the bottom and dug our own foxholes for the night. We put two rings round, we had an outer ring of defence and an inner ring. If anybody came to the outer ring, that was all right, we could let them come through and the inner ring would deal with it. They couldn't get back out again, so we had them well trapped. This was done under heavy fire, we were really getting shot up at the time. *Sergeant Bert Fitt, B Coy, 2nd Norfolks*

Inside the perimeter Captain John Mather organized the Regimental Aid Post (RAP) to deal with the casualties as they were brought in.

We arrived where we could go no further with the Japs ahead and around. We came across this Japanese depressed area in the ground which had been their first aid place. In the base of it there were narrow dugouts enough to lay a chap in. We dug more holes of course. But it was raining, God it was wet! With it being so wet, you dug a hole and it filled up with water. You couldn't really put chaps in there – but you had to because you'd got to keep them down. We had capes and things to keep some of the water off them, but I'm afraid a lot of them were in a bad way as regards comfort. *Captain John Mather, Medical Officer, HQ Coy, 2nd Norfolks*

The Japanese held Norfolk Bunker position dominated any possible direct route down the road to Jotsoma. This meant that the many wounded were trapped in the Regimental Aid Post with no chance of evacuation back along the tortuous route that they had come. It also meant that the battalion could not receive ammunition or supplies except by the medium of parachute drops. The Royal Scots who should have been the 'follow through' were already assigned to covering any possible attack from the high ground to their rear which they had so recently vacated. In these circumstance it was considered crucial to make some kind of attack to try and capture this thorn in their side while the Japanese garrison was still weak and disorganized by the loss of most of GPT Ridge. Therefore John Howard's friend, Lieutenant David Glasse, was ordered into a dangerous speculative attack with his dismounted Carrier Platoon. As the battalion lay only a few yards away from the bunker in a direct line between it and the gun line, Glasse had to make a rush frontal attack without artillery support.

David gave me his watch and said, "Take that and write to Louise, won't you and see that she gets this." I said, "We're going to see you again shortly, David!" "I doubt it! I doubt it!" He just knew he was going to get killed. Off they went. They over-ran it, David Glasse got killed and they couldn't hold it because they were shot off it again by other bunkers below. They had quite a lot of casualties and the rest came back. The order of the day then was dig in where you are, deal with casualties and that'd be it for the moment. *Lieutenant Sam Hornor, Signal Officer, HQ Coy, 2nd Norfolks*

The bodies of the dead and wounded were left scattered across the

A fearsome prospect – a Japanese bunker at Kohima.

battlefield. Many of the officers and NCOs were at the forefront of efforts to organise the collection and rescue of the men who had fought under them.

> Old 'Winkie' Fitt came down to ask for volunteers. We went down to this big bunker to try and rescue some people. This lad was crying and everytime we made a movement, so the blooming Japs must have shot him again. But we couldn't see where it was coming from or where the chap was. *Bugler Bert May, HQ Coy, 2nd Norfolks*

Medical Officer John Mather did incredible work crawling time and time again into No Mans Land to bandage up emergency cases to try to keep them alive until the stretcher bearers could get to them.

> Major Twidle was hit by a piece of flying shrapnel and his tummy was opened, his guts were hanging out. He was out on the

perimeter and he was under fire, the Japs were there. You had to crawl to get to him if you wanted to remain alive. I got to him, kept down and I was able to push his innards back in. I sprinkled him with sulphominide powder, put a big dressing on his tummy, bound him up and gave him small amounts of cold water. I gave him morphine of course. I had to look after him like that for awhile because there was no way to get him out. He was conscious, I asked him how he was and I told him we'd get him away as soon as possible but there was no way just now. I went out to him again in an hour or two's time and he seemed fairly comfortable. It lasted 12 or more hours and then we got him away, carried him without lifting him much – as painlessly as possible. I didn't know what was wrong inside him, you couldn't see for one thing. *Captain John Mather, Medical Officer, HQ Coy, 2nd Norfolks*

Roger Twidle

Mather did not see himself as a hero, but he was acting in the highest traditions of the Royal Army Medical Corps in putting the lives of others before his own.

I wasn't a nervous sort, when there was a job to do, you'd got to do it and that was it! You didn't have time to think about other things. *Captain John Mather, Medical Officer, HQ Coy, 2nd Norfolks*

The Norfolks had won a notable victory but, as is often the case, it did not appear like that to the men who crouched in their slit trenches during that night.

We'd dug our foxholes and the next morning they were half full of water. It rained all night, it was a miserable night. We'd had a hard, very hard day and a heck of a fight coming down there. All in all I think the spirits of the blokes were getting a bit down. But when they realized they had lost nearly all their senior officers and a lot of other people wounded, I think they all had the feeling the same as I did, "We'll annihilate them, come what may we're going to annihilate the Japanese". I think they all had that feeling and that raised their spirits a bit. *Sergeant Bert Fitt, B Coy, 2nd Norfolks*

In these circumstance Robert Scott's larger than life persona was truly invaluable in maintaining the morale of his isolated battalion and bringing back some perspective – next to him most Japanese were small!

He wasn't a man who just went and got in a dug-out, and stayed there. Oh no, he got out, he went round his positions to make sure that everything was covered and he spoke to people as he went round. I admired the man for it. He was a great soldier, one of the finest soldiers you could ever meet. I always said that he was one of those men who should have had the VC. *Sergeant Bert Fitt, B Coy, 2nd Norfolks*

His blustering and bellowing worked. The soldier in his cold wet slit trench felt himself gain in confidence.

Suddenly Robert Scott comes along. There we are crouched down in our holes. Scott said to us, "Come on you chaps, there's no need to be afraid, you are better than those little yellow bastards!" *Private Dick Fiddament, 2nd Norfolks*

Everyone seems to have responded to his influence.

onel Robert Scott

Two minutes with him and a man's fears were calmed. The mud and the wet didn't matter – nor did the Japs. His bravery was magnificent, that always inspires soldiers and the fact that he was still the same chap he'd always been. Most people rather tend to change in battle but Robert didn't – he was still the same awkward bugger! He was about six foot two but very big with it – huge bottom! He was covered in mud but then so were the rest of us. His huge boots on his large feet, covered in mud, looked even bigger. His trousers were covered in dried blood – he'd stabbed a Japanese at some stage so I was told. He had grenades, a pistol and his dagger hanging round his huge waistline. He'd acquired a silk Japanese flag which he was using as a scarf. Like the rest of us he had four or five days of beard which is never very pre-possessing. He had a bandaged head, his tin hat had a ragged bullet hole. "Oooh, I've got this bloody lumbago, I can't get up!" He had a long stick to lean on, a headache, in a vile temper – enjoying himself wildly. "Take cover, you silly buggers, we're being shelled! Everybody down – except me! I can't, I've got lumbago, but the buggers can't get me!" That was very cheering. "Oh dear!" he'd say, "We're all going to be killed!" Well the way he said it – it didn't matter! *Captain John Howard, Intelligence Officer, HQ, 4th Brigade*

Scott had in fact been hit a glancing blow across the head and had responded in typical fashion.

When he got hit, scalped, he shook his fist at the Japanese lines. He said, "The biggest bloke on the damn position and you couldn't get him! If you were in my bloody battalion, I'd take your proficiency pay away!" *Sergeant Bert Fitt, B Coy, 2nd Norfolks*

The total casualties suffered by the battalion in capturing GPT Ridge consisted of 3 officers killed, 5 wounded and 19 other ranks killed with 50 wounded.

On 5 May the battalion had to endure the concentrated attentions of the Japanese snipers.

Conder got hit. They had snipers every damn where and there was no way in which you could point out exactly where they were. They kept picking off people all over, but I was lucky in that I didn't lose any of my people on the 5th. I kept them under cover as much as I possibly could and I forbade any of them to move around the position. I kept a sharp lookout and told them to keep looking out to see if they could detect where these snipers were. I moved around from one position to another to pass on anything that was happening, or was going to happen. They shot at me, but I didn't care. *Sergeant Bert Fitt, B Coy, 2nd Norfolks*

After taking Major Hatch back for treatment, Hazell had dropped into the first cover he could overnight in his platoon area. Next morning he discovered he was in a very tight situation. The hole he occupied was about 4′ 6″ deep but half full of water and lay on the line of the track which ran up GPT Ridge.

When it got first light a crowd of Japs had got in our perimeter, up in the trees on either side of this track. I think I was the best target they could see. Fortunately when they first fired the shots came over my shoulder and landed in front of me, 'Bang, bang, bang'. I ducked straight away and thought, "Jesus, where did they come from?" So I put my hat on my rifle and poked it up. Another volley of shots came over which I thought was rather amusing. So I was sitting there in my hole doing this, up and down. Every time I did it over came four shots. I'd taken my pouches off and put them on the ground behind me. Suddenly there was the most deafening bang and I got covered in dirt that came down in my ears and all down my tunic. I thought, "Crikey! They've put a mortar on me now!" Anyway I carried on popping my hat up and down and then suddenly I felt cramp developing in my left leg. I knew then that I'd got about a couple of minutes to do something pretty drastic. I popped my hat up, over came the shots. I stuck my head up quick, looked around, I could see some bushes over there. I waited for a few moments, popped the hat up again, over came the shots and I rolled over into these bushes. They didn't afford an awful lot of cover, but obviously they couldn't see me because nobody shot at me from then onwards. I lay out flat there for half an hour and never moved. While I was laying there A Company that were in reserve way back up the ridge had spotted the problem and sent four Bren gunners who just sprayed the trees. That was that! I then went back to pick up my pouches. The bang that I'd heard was one of the shots had hit them and blown all the grenades up. My water bottle had gone – everything had gone. The only thing I was in possession of then was a rifle, I had nothing else. But there was plenty of wounded and dead so I soon made good any deficiencies. *Sergeant Fred Hazell, D Coy 2nd Norfolks*

Hazel had been lucky but all day there was a constant drip of casualties as the snipers patiently waited for someone to make a mistake by showing themselves long enough for a clear shot.

In the slit trench next to me was a chap, Corporal Payne, 'Dolly' we called him, I don't know why. We were 'standing to' and I heard a shot, we knew automatically that was a sniper. He'd poked his head up, he was quite a tall chap and this sniper shot him. The bullet entered the right hand side of his forehead. The front had gone, his brain was visible. We got to him, we put him down in the trench, covered him with a monsoon cape. He actually said, "You might as well fill the bloody hole up". There's thousands of things that you forget and yet incidents like this it's as though it was yesterday. You can see him as though he's here now. *Private Dick Fiddament, 2nd Norfolks*

Sergeant Robinson was hit and in that moment found that real life was not as portrayed in Hollywood movies.

All this John Wayne business when they just grab their arm and go down gently. That doesn't happen – you feel as though you've been kicked by a horse. My leg went straight from under me and of course I fell to the ground. I didn't know what had happened, I'd got a nice hole in my trousers, so I tore it to see what had happened. I put my field dressing on my wound – just above my knee on the left leg. I tied it as well, as tight as I could. I was bleeding fairly badly. They'd got their eyes on me, so discretion was the better part of valour. I crawled away to get a bit more cover. It was difficult pushing myself along with one leg, the left one was useless. I waited for any help that was forthcoming. *Sergeant William Robinson, A Coy, 2nd Norfolks*

He was carried back to the RAP where he received very little treatment as the medics strained to deal with the more serious cases.

It was raining, raining very heavy. The side of the little dugout that I was in became jelly and the mud slid back and covered over you. Mind you, that kept you warm! So I'd got this bit of half blanket over the bottom part of my leg, because I wanted to keep it as clean as possible in all that mud. My leg was numb, very, very numb. I didn't know to what extent I'd been hit and what the damage was – I had visions of being a cripple, I think anybody would be thinking that. I was there probably a couple or three days. I didn't get any treatment there at all. It was continually raining, I thought it was never going to stop. You didn't want to go to the toilet strangely enough, because you'd had no food, nothing much. Everybody was doing their best, it was a situation that you accepted. There was a lot of wounded. *Sergeant William Robinson, A Coy, 2nd Norfolks*

The numbers of the wounded built up in the RAP over several days. Their situation was depressing in the extreme. Sergeant Ben Macrae was sniped through the chest and even his naturally cheerful and optimistic nature was weighed down.

I tried to get some blooming sleep. I was desperate for sleep, but you couldn't get it, because our own mortars were firing and there was bangs going off all the time. I got a blanket, covered my head right over and tried to sleep. Sergeant Major Wylie, come up, "Oh, what's the matter, I thought you were dead!" I said, "Not yet!" What dead we had were covered up with a blanket. All they had was a morphia injection, that's all they could do and put a dressing on. They couldn't do nothing else. The Doctor said, "You're not coughing up blood?" I said, "No!" "Oh", he said, "your lungs are all right then, it's gone straight through. Luckily we don't think it's hit anything vital – if you cough up blood let me know instantly!" I was wet, I began to feel cold and your nerves got to you. You could have sat down and cried your eyes out. Which a lot of blokes did – they got so low spirited with it all. You were hungry, cold and wet, you thought, "When am I going to get out of here?" You didn't, you couldn't! *Sergeant Ben Macrae, Carrier Platoon, HQ Coy, 2nd Norfolks*

Mather was of course aware that his patients were suffering but there was little he could do in the circumstances.

It was awful conditions for them, everything wet and sodden. You tend to try to keep people warm – well with cold water soaking their clothes it wasn't easy. But look at Twidle, he did very well on the whole – he must have been a bit wet. Of course he was sensible, he wasn't an idiot he just did as he was told. Keep dry and still, not eat or drink anything other than what we gave him. Of course I didn't know what had happened inside him and he was lucky that nothing had. *Captain John Mather, Medical Officer, HQ Coy, 2nd Norfolks*

As evening fell Captain Jack Randle, who had taken over the command of B Company, took out a reconnaissance patrol to investigate the exact location and composition of the string of inter–connected bunkers which made up Norfolk Bunker. Fitt went with him.

That night we went out on a patrol, to make contact with the enemy on the right of Norfolk Bunker immediately in between us and Kohima. As far as reconnaissance was concerned we did in actual fact make contact, but we were lucky, we got back without losing anybody. We just carried on until somebody shot at us, and when they shot at us, well we had to just give a quick dive to ground to observe what was ahead of us, roughly where this had happened. *Sergeant Bert Fitt, B Coy, 2nd Norfolks*

Randle held his company 'O' Group to brief his platoon commanders. Fitt was commanding 9 Platoon.

The plan was to attack Norfolk Bunker from the front. They called it 'the bunker', in actual fact it consisted of about seven or eight different bunkers. My platoon was the spearhead to the centre, they had 12 Platoon to the right. There was only the two platoons really to go forward. Then they had the reserve platoon which was 10 Platoon and a Support Platoon which was under the command of Captain Davies. That consisted of machine gunners and so forth from the Carrier Platoon. He raked up his own support, Captain Davies did. It was an out and out frontal attack, because we were going in at dawn, at first light and we thought at the time that was the most obvious way in which we were going to take it because we'd got to climb up a hill to take this bunker. The trees had all been shelled by people before us, and all the branches had been knocked off. There was very little cover. *Sergeant Bert Fitt, B Coy, 2nd Norfolks*

Davies and Randle talked quietly together that night.

We talked about our families. What we planned to do after the war. All sorts of things. His son was born on the same day as mine and we wondered what they'd be like. He said this is a bloody awful shambles and we talked over what we were going to do. *Captain Dickie Davies, Carrier Platoon, HQ Coy, 2nd Norfolks*

B Company moved on to the start line, ready for the attack just before dawn.

Captain Randle came up and he laid beside me. He said "I've seen all the horrible things that's happened to me in my past". I said "So have I!" I think that he had an idea that he would not come out of that attack. *Sergeant Bert Fitt, B Coy, 2nd Norfolks*

Supported by the covering fire of the Carrier Platoon Bren guns and mortars they moved off into a hail of Japanese bullets.

We moved and we got about half way to the base of the hill. Captain Randle had already been hit at least twice before we ever got to the bottom of the hill. He staggered twice, that told me that he had been hit fairly heavily in the upper part of his body. I shouted to him, told him to go down and leave it to me, because you could see that he'd lost blood. He said, "No! You take that left hand bunker, I'm going to take this right hand one". They were two light machine-gun posts and they were carving up the company terrible. *Sergeant Bert Fitt, B Coy, 2nd Norfolks*

Fitt managed to get in close to his prey and dealt with it in text book fashion.

I got mine by coming up underneath and before they could spin a gun onto me I had

Jack Randle VC

191

The climatic moment of the attack on Norfolk Bunker 6 May 1944. Randle is facing the bunker whilst Fitt makes his vain attempt to get across in time to help his gallant officer.

a grenade in the bunker. You see they didn't realise that I was coming up underneath them I moved so quick. It had a protection cover over it. I managed to get a grenade in, pushed it in through the slit and after four seconds 'WHHOOFF' it went up. I knew that anybody inside that bunker was either dead or knocked out. I immediately spun right because I thought I could have got to where Captain Randle was before anything happened. *Sergeant Bert Fitt, B Coy, 2nd Norfolks*

192

Tragically he was too late for Randle had reached his moment of destiny just some 20 yards away. Fitt was left a helpless spectator for the final act of heroism which earned Jack Randle imperishable fame and a posthumous VC.

> As I turned right I saw Captain Randle at the bunker entrance. He had a grenade he was going to release into the bunker and he had his protective weapon with him. I just stood there, I couldn't do a thing to save him. If he could have held out for about three minutes I would have got on top of the bunker and knocked it out without getting hurt. But unfortunately he had been hit again at point blank range. As he was going down he threw his grenade into the bunker and he sealed the bunker entrance with his own body. So that nobody could shoot from it. But he had in actual fact got the occupants – killed them. I thought to myself, "That's the end of Captain Randle". *Sergeant Bert Fitt, B Coy, 2nd Norfolks*

Fitt still had work to do for the two bunkers were just the start of the Japanese defence system. He rushed forward another 15 yards to the next bunker.

> The bloke was just going to have his breakfast because he had a tin of curry there opened. I threw my grenade – that was open that bunker – and I shot him at the same time. That was where I used my last round of ammunition. *Sergeant Bert Fitt, B Coy, 2nd Norfolks*

Still he plunged on but when he reached the next bunker he encountered a Japanese soldier who came out to meet him man to man.

> Well he knew damn well that if he stayed in there, he was going to get a grenade in, so he had to come out. He came out of his back door of the bunker and he was behind me. I didn't see him when he fired. He shot me and he got me through the side of the face, underneath under my jaw. He took my top teeth out and fractured my maxilla and the bullet burnt along the side of my nose. It felt like just as if somebody with a clenched fist had just hit me. I wouldn't say that it hurt in the terms of being hurt. It didn't hurt me as much as what a good punch had done in the past in a fight. I just spat out a handful of teeth and I spun round. He was only a matter of a few paces away, facing me. He had a rifle and bayonet and I had a light machine gun. I pressed the trigger and I'd got no ammunition, I'd used it. As he came towards me, I had that feeling that it was either me or him. When you get to hand to hand fighting like that, you realize that you or he's going to get killed, so what do you do? You close in and you hope for the best. I was a good instructor in unarmed combat, I could go hand to hand or meet anybody with a rifle and bayonet, I knew how to deal with them and I could do it. I let him come and I crashed the light

machine gun into his face. I threw it straight in his face. Before he hit the ground I had my hand on his windpipe and I literally tried to tear it out. It wouldn't come – if I could have got his windpipe out, I would have twisted it round his neck. We were tossing over on the ground. I managed to get his bayonet from his rifle and I finished him with that. He was the one that died, not me. *Sergeant Bert Fitt, B Coy, 2nd Norfolks*

This elemental confrontation was not the end of the battle.

I stood up and I had a call from 12 Platoon telling me that they were pinned down from another bunker, which I couldn't see. I asked them whereabouts it was and they told me as best they could. I threw a grenade, it went over the top and a chap who could see it yelled back a correction. I threw a second one, it was short, hit the ground before it got to the open bunker and it bounced straight into the bunker – the occupants in there obviously were killed as well. There was still more bunkers over the other side. One of my corporals, Corporal Sculforte, he spotted another bunker, which was slightly over the crest to the left. He started going towards it. I yelled to him and tried to stop him, but I couldn't. He continued, went about a further four or five paces and he was shot down. *Sergeant Bert Fitt, B Coy, 2nd Norfolks*

Fitt's platoon were on top of the position but they had not captured all of the bunker complex. At this point Davies brought up his platoon to consolidate the position.

I was told that as soon as I got a signal from the bunker I was to advance on to the bunker. My great worry at that time was that I wouldn't see them. My Bren guns were shooting like blazes and I was terrified they'd come out on the bunker and I'd shoot them. Nothing happened. I sent a message back to battalion headquarters, "Shall I advance?" I never got an answer. By this time I knew that I had to get forward, I'd got to consolidate, so I took my gamble. When I got down there on the bunker there was only Fitt and about sixteen chaps there. Fitt had a bad wound in the face. He was very shaken from the pure physical effort. He shouted, "Randle's killed!" *Captain Dickie Davies, Carrier Platoon, HQ Coy, 2nd Norfolks*

Davies recognized that Fitt was in full control of the situation and did not stand on his rank.

Captain Davies came up and I'd been hit, oh it must have been two hours previous, I'd been bleeding heavily and the front of me was pretty red with blood. I was getting weak and I said to him, "Well you'd better take over now, Sir". Davies said, "No, you consolidate the position, you know what's going on more than me, I'll do anything you ask me to do". He was our support platoon. I told him, "Look, I'll have to sit down!" I went and I sat just inside an old bunker, I don't know whether it was Japanese or it wasn't, I couldn't care less at the time. I sat in there and they put a field bandage around my head to make it look a bit respectable. *Sergeant Bert Fitt, B Coy, 2nd Norfolks*

Davies and his men set to work in trying to deal with the Japanese bunkers that Fitt had identified on the other side of the hillock facing Jail Hill.

There were other bunkers who were shooting further down the ridge towards the road. We couldn't throw grenades at them so what you did was you got your bayonet out and made a hole in the top. Pulled the ring out of your grenade and dropped it in through the hole. There were shots going all over the place. I picked up a Sten gun and I thought I'd carry that instead of a rifle. Four Japanese got out of one of these bunkers we'd been dropping grenades in and ran down the hill. I pressed the trigger and nothing bloody well happened – my Sten gun jammed! They always jammed – a useless weapon. I threw it at them – I was so annoyed. *Second Lieutenant Dickie Davies, Carrier Platoon, HQ Coy, 2nd Norfolks*

Not every one could cope with the stress of such vicious combat in the manner of the hardened 'Winkie' Fitt. Ironically one of his men cracked after the main danger was over.

I never had any kind of nervous reaction at all. But some of the men did. One chap he lost his nerve, he wanted to run forward after the Japanese, wanted to go after them on his own. He just went into high hysterics like. I hit him to quieten him down. That was the only thing I could do to stop him, otherwise he would have run out and he would have got killed. I punched him, told him to be quiet and pull himself together – and he did. He'd come through it, done an excellent job right the way through – but he lost his nerve at the finish, just cracked. That's a horrible thing to happen, and if you're near them, the only thing you can do is hit them to stop them. *Sergeant Bert Fitt, B Coy, 2nd Norfolks*

Eventually Fitt was evacuated back to the RAP where he met Colonel Scott and Dr Mather.

The first words the colonel said to me was, "They got you then, Fitt?" I said "That's right, Sir!" He said, "Let's have a look!" The Medical Officer removed the field dressing. Colonel Scott stood in front of me and he went, "Ho, ho, ho! You never were any bloody oil painting!" *Sergeant Bert Fitt, B Coy, 2nd Norfolks*

John Howard also saw Fitt as he moved back.

I saw 'Winkie' Fitt, he was slightly wounded and he was being evacuated through brigade headquarters. I greeted him as he came up to the field ambulance place and we exchanged a few words.

He said, "I've had far worse bloody noses than this boxing and they're trying to evacuate me!" I said, "Well, 'Winkie', you'll have to go!" I myself think that if he'd been killed, instead of Jack, the VC would have been the other way round. They were in it together. *Captain John Howard, Intelligence Officer, HQ, 4th Brigade*

Fitt was to be awarded the Distinguished Conduct Medal. Davies was left to consolidate the captured bunkers. At first he tried to get in the wounded and dead.

We went out and got one or two of the wounded in. I saw David Glasse's body and my batman and I got him up. I took his top, my batman took the bottom and his body fell in two. A machine gun had gone straight across his tummy. Then we were getting Jack in, but a message came from battalion headquarters to say that, "Nobody is to go out, we've had too many casualties – the wounded will have to be left". We were on top and he was down below, it was a fairly steep bunker, seven or eight feet high at least. *Captain Dickie Davies, Carrier Platoon, HQ Coy, 2nd Norfolks*

The Norfolks spent a grim night for they expected the Japanese to counter-attack at any moment.

Towards the evening we had a mist. We were in our slit trenches during that night and the Japs had put tins out with stones in them. We heard these tins rattling and the Japanese were shouting because they wanted us to shout back, "Are you there Tommy?" It was horrible, it really was, I was very scared. We were soaking wet, we had no cover. *Captain Dickie Davies, Carrier Platoon, HQ Coy, 2nd Norfolks*

After a while Davies took shelter in the main bunker.

It was full of Jap dead. They sent us down some bully beef and my batman said, "Let's have it!" I said, "OK!" He got his hankie out of his pocket – it was filthy you can imagine what it was like – a khaki hankie. He put it over the tummy of a dead Japanese, just over his bare tummy. He pulled this warm bully beef out with his finger, put it on a biscuit and said, "Here you are, Sir!" I couldn't eat it, I was sick! *Captain Dickie Davies, Carrier Platoon, HQ Coy, 2nd Norfolks*

Although the whole of the Norfolk Bunker had not been captured, it had been at least in part neutralized and soon contact was established with the 4/1st Ghurka Rifles, part of the 33rd Indian Brigade, which had been moved up into the area between Two Tree Hill and GPT Ridge. As a result it was possible to open a direct track down to Jotsoma which finally allowed the casualties to be evacuated over the next couple of days. The wounded were aware that there was little chance of their wounds actually getting them right back to 'Blighty' – England.

I knew I hadn't got a 'Blighty' one – to get a 'Blighty' one you

Artillery bombardment bursting just beyond the British front lines. IWM IND 3434

had to be really hit, mostly legs. A bullet right through the ankle, that was a 'Blighty' one because you couldn't do much with that, it was a long drawn out job. You might have a stiff ankle or stiff knee for the rest of your life. For a 'Blighty' one you had to be really hit and I'm not sure that I wanted that! *Sergeant Ben Macrae, Carrier Platoon, HQ Coy, 2nd Norfolks*

By this time in the tropical conditions the minor leg wounds suffered by Robinson had putrefied badly.

I was carried down on a stretcher. My leg was bad by this stage, putrefying. Eventually when I got down to the bottom the medical officer looked at it and he said, "Well you owe your life to these!" I said, "What's that?" And I was maggoty – they'd cleaned it... I was most upset, the appearance of it. I didn't want it as my leg it was so horrific. I thought, "If you've got to take it off, take it off – I don't want that!" That's as bad as I felt. *Sergeant William Robinson, A Coy, 2nd Norfolks*

His leg was saved. Many were less fortunate.

There were a fair number of corpses but they were cleared up every night. The Regimental Police had the job of burying the dead every night. Which wasn't a very pleasant task. I could hear them bringing their hearts up while they were doing the job. *Sergeant Fred Hazell, D Coy, 2nd Norfolks*

****

During the 4th Brigade's long march on their right hook to GPT Ridge the 5th Brigade had made some progress towards their own objectives on the left of the 2nd Division front as they moved moved slowly towards Naga Village. Meanwhile the 6th Brigade had

achieved some success in their parallel attacks on the Kohima Ridge in the centre. At great cost the Japanese had been pushed back from the area around the DC's bungalow and positions had been re–established on part of FSD Hill, although the Japanese held firm on Kuki Picquet. Unfortunately the capture of what remained of Norfolk Bunker on the reverse slopes of the hillock at the end of GPT Ridge was still absolutely crucial for it commanded the approaches to much of the rest of the hills that together formed the Kohima Ridge. Despite reverses the Japanese positions remained formidable. The framework of inter-locking supporting fire at which the Japanese excelled was intact and the concealed machine guns caused much execution amongst the attacking British and Indian troops. As a result a further attempt to capture the Norfolk Bunker was ordered to be carried out by the 4/1st Ghurkas on 7 May. The attack was a complete failure as the sheer volume of fire, not only from Norfolk Bunker, but from the rest of the Kohima defensive complex, undermined the resolve of the Gurkhas to such an extent that the officers charged to their deaths almost alone. Whilst observing this failure Brigadier William Goshen was killed by a sniper.

Goschen came down with Robert Scott, full of red things on their hats, silly arses! I said, "Excuse me, Sir, there are snipers there, could you get down!" But he was a Guardsman and he still thought it was an exercise! You know – a Guardsman wouldn't get down – he didn't and unfortunately got killed. *Captain Dickie Davies, D Coy, 2nd Norfolks*

This left no less a person than Lieutenant-Colonel Robert Scott as acting Brigadier!

Of course he wouldn't come to brigade headquarters – not bloody likely! "John, you'll come down to the battalion." He didn't want any of the other brigade staff there. I virtually was the brigade staff. There wasn't very much to do really. The Royal Scots and the Norfolks were busy in contact with the enemy very much a static situation apart from these odd attacks which petered out. *Captain John Howard, Intelligence Officer, HQ, 4th Brigade*

Still the problem of Norfolk Bunker remained and in fact machine guns based there had been partially instrumental in breaking up an all out attack by 1st Battalion, Queen's Royal West Surrey Regiment on Jail Hill which lay directly across the Kohima road from GPT Ridge. On 8 May, Major General John Grover arrived to assess the situation and congratulated the Norfolks on their achievements so far. He naturally noticed Scott's head wound received on 4 May. Grover would not have been human if he had not commented on it in view of Scott's argument with him before the operation commenced over the relative merits of steel helmets and bush hats.

If he hadn't had a tin hat he'd have been dead. It went straight through the tin hat, knocked him out slightly and sort of whizzed across the skull as bullets do. But if it hadn't been a tin hat there which sort of slowed it down he would probably have been dead. That delighted the Divisional Commander! When he first saw him he said, "Well Robert, are you going to apologize to me now about tin hats!" *Lieutenant Sam Hornor, Signal Officer, HQ Coy, 2nd Norfolks*

It is perhaps fortunate that Scott's reply is not recorded! Perhaps more to the point Grover offered Scott the chance to give his men two days' rest in Dimapur before being sent in to capture Jail Hill. Scott was wary of pulling out of the line for such a short rest. He felt it was not long enough to allow men to recover, but might instead allow morbid reflection on the casualties suffered, and that this would actually be prejudicial to good morale. It was therefore decided that the battalion would remain in the line where they were, with a view to consolidating the position on GPT Ridge and, with any luck, finally eradicating the remnants of Norfolk Bunker.

Next day Brigadier Jack Theobalds arrived, freshly promoted from his former role as second in command of 5th Brigade. Scott reverted to commanding the Norfolks. One consequence of this change-over in Brigadiers was a change in 'shaving policy'. This caused considerable personal embarrassment for John Howard.

We all had four or five days of beard then because 'Willie' Goschen, Guardsman though he was, said, "We will not shave!" It was fashionable because the Chindits, Wingate's lot, didn't shave. Then when Jack Theobalds came along he said, "The brigade will shave!" I was directed to go down and see the Norfolks to give them the Brigadier's oral instructions to shave. Well of course I had to shave first, I found a razor somewhere. So I went down still covered in mud and God knows what else, with not much sleep for a week. I arrived at the Norfolks and my friends greeted me as a gilded staff officer because I'd shaved. *Captain John Howard, Intelligence Officer, HQ, 4th Brigade*

Such visits to the front line positions were not without risk as Howard found out.

We arrived almost simultaneously with a burst of three inch mortar bombs from the Japanese. I hopped into a very small and shallow slit trench already full of mud, Oscar Whitaker and somebody else. As I did so there was a swish and a bomb went off on the ground about two feet away. I had just made it in time. Several more bombs fell round the crowded area. Several men were hit, two were killed.[16] *Captain John Howard, Intelligence Officer, HQ, 4th Brigade*

It was decided that some form of direct artillery support was essential if the rest of Norfolk Bunker was to be captured.

Two anti-tank guns had been taken to bits and man handled up to the Norfolk positions with great difficulty and very slowly. The enemy positions were a few yards from the regiment's forward foxholes and it was impossible to use conventional artillery support with our own men so close. It was intended to move the anti-tank guns into firing positions about an hour before dark; the positions having been prepared the previous night. They would then fire over open sights at a range of about forty yards and blast the Japs' bunkers to atoms.[17] *Captain John Howard, Intelligence Officer, HQ, 4th Brigade*

C Company, which was then under the command of Captain 'Dickie' Davies, was to infiltrate Norfolk Bunker position. The two 6 pounder anti-tank guns were dragged into positions and were ready for action on the night of 9 May.

They ended up about ten foot to my right and a couple of yards in front of me. I had a grandstand seat of the whole affair. You could see the bullets hitting the shield of this gun, just like hail. Of course the two lads who ran the gun out hadn't got any ammunition and the two lads with the box of ammunition couldn't get out because it was under constant fire. In the end the two lads who ran the gun out nipped back. I got a message on the phone, "Apart from your other duties, don't let the gun fall into enemy hands!" *Sergeant Fred Hazell, D Coy, 2nd Norfolks*

The other gun did manage to open fire and stuck to it although the gun shield was riddled with bullets which meant that they were lucky to get away with just one or two casualties. Howard was with Scott and Theobalds as they awaited the results of the attack in Robert Scott's 'headquarters'.

The Brigadier, Robert and I sat in Robert's ridiculous shallow sleeping hole and waited on the telephone. The platoon made their objective with only one casualty. A signaller with a telephone followed them. The distance of the assault had been about fifty yards only. For a while it looked all right. But it was not. In a few minutes grenades were busting by the dozen on the new position and on the original bunker where Jack Randle's body still lay with those of many more of his company. Sergeant Gilbert commanding the platoon was killed. The Japs were crawling up to counter-attack under cover of sustained grenade fire. Several more men of the weak platoon were hit, some killed. Bill Brown, now Second-in-Command of the Battalion, was at Norfolk Bunker and he told Robert that he thought that if the platoon stayed there it would be destroyed.[18] *Captain John Howard, Intelligence Officer, HQ, 4th Brigade*

The Brigadier and Scott bowed to the inevitable and the platoon was withdrawn. Next day they and several of the brigade staff met for morning conference right in front of Norfolk Bunker to decide what was to be done next.

> He came down looking all very spic and span, with his red braided cap on and so forth. He was with the Brigade Major and four or five others. He knelt down alongside my hole and said, "I thought I'd come up and see where all the action is, how are things going?" I said, "Well apart from, grenades, it's fairly quiet at the moment but keep your eyes open for grenades. I wouldn't stand there if I was you! In fact there's a grenade coming now!" They were firing these grenades because they came up quite slowly and it was heading our way. There was a slit trench just behind me, a fairly long one and they all jammed in. Behind it there was a tree stump, about six foot back and about eight foot tall. I looked over my shoulder and I saw this bloody grenade hit the top of this tree stump and bounce back into the trench. *Sergeant Fred Hazell, D Coy, 2nd Norfolks*

Scott was unscathed, but the staff officers suffered awfully. Theobalds himself was carried back to Mather in the RAP but it was hopeless.

> One of his friends was talking to him and the Brigadier got his wallet and said, "Send that to my wife and tell her she was the last one I was thinking of". I heard that. He was hit in the back – probably spinal cord. It paralysed him. *Captain John Mather, Medical Officer, HQ Coy, 2nd Norfolks*

Theobalds was evacuated but died on 16 May. Once more Scott was in temporary command of the brigade.

The failure finally to deal with Norfolk Bunker meant that the main attacks launched on the remaining Japanese positions on DIS Ridge, FSD Ridge and Jail Hill on 11 May were seriously undermined as the Japanese crossfire once again cost precious lives. Yet other regiments had proud traditions and they too could sometimes succeed against all the odds. The 1st Queens supported by the 4/1st Ghurkas, although under fire from every side, nevertheless managed to establish themselves on Jail Hill. The one advantage they had was that the freeing of the DC's bungalow area had made it gradually easier for tanks to get forward to lend direct support to the hard pressed infantry. On 12 May the attacks were renewed with ever increasing armoured support and the Japanese resistance began to crack. The positions on Jail Hill were much improved whilst the Royal Berkshires were successful in clearing most of FSD Ridge.

As it was obvious that for the moment at least the Norfolks had shot their bolt, it was decided that the 1st Royal Scots would make the final attack on the Norfolk Bunker. However the Japanese forces were also at the end of their tether. At the end of insecure supply lines, wracked by severe casualties from the constant British attacks, as they gradually lost control, so their lethal crossfire lost its potency and their formerly inviolable bunkers were left in isolation. On 13 May they withdrew from all their positions on the eastern slopes of Jail Hill, Kuki Picquet, FSD and DIS Ridges. On 14 and 15 May the Royal Scots attacked with the support of tanks and at last Norfolk Bunker was over-run. Thus the fighting ended on Kohima Ridge. The Japanese remained in strength in the northern Naga Village sector, and withdrew the rest of their forces to new positions on Aradura Spur from which they hoped to prevent relief forces passing down the road to Imphal.

Japanese prisoners were a rare sight in this most ruthless of battles.

CHAPTER ELEVEN

Aradura Spur

For two weeks the Norfolks remained in position on GPT Ridge metaphorically licking their wounds and waiting for the next advance. Patrols were sent out exploring the Aradura Nala and probing the extent of the Japanese defences. They were therefore still in contact with the Japanese throughout the period. Sniping had gone on right from the start and the Norfolks had their own specialists who took the Japanese on at their own game.

There was a tricklet of water coming down the rocks and we found out, whilst going ourselves to get some water, that the Japs had been going there as well. Me and Billy Williams said, "Right, we'll get up the trees and line up where we can watch this water spout – when Japs come we can give them a surprise!" Consequently we used to go out last thing at night and get up a tree. Then we'd sit there and wait until the next morning when the Japs came in the first daylight to get their water. Sometimes two or three would come with their big water cans. With the slow trickle of the water they had to sit there sometimes for half an hour which gave us a good chance to weigh up the situation. I had a rifle sometimes and a Bren gun sometimes. Bill would line them up with his rifle and he would give me the signal from the other tree. We had our own secret codes where we could imitate a bird. When he fired his rifle I'd fire my Bren gun so consequently you were getting in the region of 35-40 shots going into three or four, maybe six Japanese. After we shot them, some died, some didn't, some got away, some ran away screaming. You always feel sorry until you've shot somebody, but don't forget if you hadn't shot them and if you fell out that tree, they'd have shot you – that's the point, see. As a soldier you shoot to kill, because if you don't they'll kill you. You must always have that in your mind. After we fired at them we were doomed to dead silence. To stay where we were, not moving or giving our secret away. We used to put a belt round the tree and round a branch and you'd sit up there asleep. They were very thick, heavily leafed. We never went up the same tree, we never went to the same area and we went a different way back each time. One danger was getting back without getting shot by the lads so every time we came out we had a password call to get back in again. When we got nearly up to them somebody would say, "Hey up, who's that?" and we used to say, "Woodbine!" and he'd answer "Players" When we got back they used to say, "Have you filled our

William Cron

205

water bottles!" I said, "No, you'll have to drink what you've got!" We did that for ten – fifteen nights, not consecutively but spread over a time. We recorded 24 in seven days shared between us. *Private William Cron, Carrier Platoon, HQ Coy, 2nd Norfolks*

Both Private Cron and Corporal Williams were awarded the MM for their actions. The risks they took were incredible as was illustrated when Fiddament and his friends found evidence that the battalion's champion sniper, Private Crampion, the oldest man in the battalion with 27 years service, had obviously taken one risk too many.

We went forward to where he lay. He was six foot two at the very least and all you could see was maggots. He was completely obliterated it was just a mass of maggots. To me it looked like a marble statue. By that time we'd seen practically every horror that man could inflict on man, none the less the thought of maggots was repugnant – they're horrible hideous creatures. That's how he lay. *Private Dick Fiddament, 2nd Norfolks*

Billy Williams receiv *his MM from the* *Viceroy of India Fiel* *Marshal Lord Wavel*

IWM 3655

Although most of the battlefield corpses had been gathered in for burial those that remained soon rotted.

The smell, ohhh, the wind changed, the vile smell. Once you've smelled death in all its ugly form, you never forget it. I can sit quietly now and I can smell it, I really can smell it. You can lose a pal, or you see one of the enemy and within a very short time they bloat and blow up. You can hear them explode. You can hear gases coming from them. *Private Dick Fiddament, 2nd Norfolks*

During this period the cooks managed to get through and set straight to work to provide a hot meal for the men.

Within half an hour, they'd obviously pre-prepared every-thing, they were shouting out, "Grub up!" Every other man made his way back with his mess tin and got something to eat. I went up and they'd cooked a bully beef hash – bully beef, reconstituted potatoes and reconstituted onions. It was absolute ambrosia it really was. I don't think I've ever enjoyed food so much in all my life. So much so that I went back and had another helping. With hindsight it was probably about the worst thing the cooks could have produced. The following day everybody had the runs. *Sergeant Fred Hazell, D Coy, 2nd Norfolks*

The uncertain diet was not the only health hazard on GPT Ridge. The shallow graves, unrecovered corpses, difficulties in maintaining latrine discipline under fire and ever present flies, meant that dysentery soon raised its ugly head.

I was sharing a slit trench with Gerry Myler and my trousers were so awful. We smelt so awful you couldn't live with yourself, you hated yourself. We each pinched a pair of trousers from chaps who were dead. Gerry used to take a ration tin with him to the 'O'

Group because he couldn't hold it. *Captain Dickie Davies, D Coy, 2nd Norfolks*

It was a terribly debilitating disease which could bring anyone to their knees.

We had a sanitary squad busy digging latrines way back up in the trees. They were kept very busy, stripped to the waist, and as fast as they dug them the lads filled them up. Everybody had to report to the MO and we were given a glass of Epsom salts and told to go back the following day when we were given a glass of kaolin. I think the theory was that the salts flushed you out completely then the kaolin tightened you up. Although everybody had the runs I didn't, but I still went and got my ration of Epsom salts. As far as I was concerned it was a drink anyway and drinks were hard to come by. So that when I had the kaolin I think one got in the way of the other and I ended up in a terrible state! The commanding officer called for his 'O' group and I was lying in the bottom of my trench with my knees under my chin. It was drizzling, I don't think I'd ever felt so miserable in all my life. Somebody shouted down, "You're wanted at 'O' Group!" It was as much as I could do to stand up and get out of the trench. It had been drizzling for quite a time and the ground was quite uneven, with all the shelling there wasn't a blade of grass to be seen. It was all sort of slimy so I skidded about all over as I made my way across to the CO's bunker. I'd just about got there when Captain Lowe who was then promoted to adjutant, suddenly appeared from behind a tree. He said, "Where are you going?" I said, "CO's orders!" He said, "No, you're not, no! I've been watching you, you can't bloody walk, what's the point of you going to CO's orders, you're going down there!" He pointed to the MO's bunker. So I went down and I was laid out on a stretcher. He looked at my stomach which was blown up like a balloon. He scratched his head and I don't think he quite knew what to do about it. He said, "I think I'll have to evacuate you". The following morning I was evacuated, taken down the slope on a stretcher. Then I was driven to Dimapur. My stomach was blown out and I had terrific griping pains. The driver was a Sikh and he drove the ambulance flat out round all these hair pin bends. I was tossed from side to side just like a bundle of washing. Had I been wounded I'd have died from my wounds long before I got to the hospital. But it stirred my inside up so much that I'd filled my trousers and goodness knows what. By the time I got to the hospital I was in a terrible mess. It was so embarrassing because when he opened the doors there were two very attractive looking young nurses standing there to help me out. I was unshaven, unwashed and I'd filled me trousers. I didn't know what to think. Anyway they escorted me to a

The Norfolks on GPT Ridge faced the Japanese across the Nala on Aradura Ridge.

208

bathroom, gave me a big bar of soap, shaving kit, couple of nice big white towels and said, "Give us a shout when you're ready and we'll put you to bed!" I had a luxurious bath and when I shaved I just could not believe my eyes – my cheeks were hollow, my eyes were popping out. They escorted me to bed, brought me a tray and some biscuits and I fell asleep. I slept for 36 hours. *Sergeant Fred Hazell, D Coy, 2nd Norfolks*

The Japanese managed to get a 75 mm gun up into a concealed position across the valley from GPT Ridge on Aradura Spur.

They'd got one of their guns dug into the side and they started shelling us because we were exposed to them. They never fired more than one shell and then they hurriedly pulled it back into a sort of cave they'd dug to put it in. Our gunners, the first time this happened we said, "Right, range on that, put the battery down on that and see if you can get it!" But it always shot back quickly, a sort of hide and seek business. The Japs are creatures of habit and they always fired this one shot at 6 o'clock in the evening. So we altered the times of feeding so that we weren't roaming about. We stood to at five to six, every evening in our holes ready to receive artillery fire – one shot landed! Robert Scott was remarkable, he didn't like these latrines where you sat on a pole and tried to remember not to fall in – very uncomfortable. He had a thunder box constructed and mounted right in the middle of the battalion position, the highest point. At 6 o'clock every day he would mount his thunder box then shout, "Get in your bloody holes – we're all going to be killed!" He would sit there doing his stuff on his thunderbox – the effect on morale was incredible. Eventually the gunners got it, pin–pointed it and fired a complete battery on to it just as it was going to come out. *Lieutenant Sam Hornor, Signal Officer, HQ Coy, 2nd Norfolks*

Second Lieutenant Maurice Franses had recently rejoined B Company as a replacement. He had been held back with the transport during the earlier battles probably due to his relative youth. Franses was sent on a reconnaissance patrol towards the upper part of the Aradura Nala.

We went into the jungle up a little nala, a dried up little stream. I realized that wasn't a good place to go because that's where they would watch for you coming. I said to the chaps, "You'd better get up either side!". We couldn't see each other, we were separated by no more than about 10 yards either side of this gully. Then all of a sudden we were fired on. I thought that fire was coming from where our C Company were because they'd been in advance of us. We ducked and managed to avoid it. I called out, "Stop firing, C Company!" Back came the reply from the Japanese, obvious from the sound of it, it was them just mimicking, "Stop firing, C Company!" The odd, "Come on, Johnny!" Things like that. So at least we'd done a job – we knew where they were. I saw a Japanese helmet just a few feet away from me in quite thick scrub and heard a metallic tap, which I realized must be a grenade being primed. I watched for it, got my grenade ready. His missed me and I threw one back. We were quite close, in fact we were so close that he probably wouldn't normally have used a grenade. I lobbed mine in his direction. At that stage I realized that we had done all we could do and so we came out. *Second Lieutenant Maurice Franses, B Coy, 2nd Norfolks*

In preparation for the planned attack on Aradura Spur all platoon and company commanders were taken to Treasury Hill from which they could get a sight of the rear of the Japanese positions. The Norfolks and the Royal Scots were to attack frontally on 27 May supported by an artillery concentration and an attack from the 6th Brigade who had been moved right round to a position higher up facing Aradura village itself. It was a severely weakened battalion that received these orders as only 14 officers and 366 other ranks were fit to take their place in the line. Many of these men were suffering from advanced fatigue and dysentery.

I remember thinking when I looked at it, "This is a straight-forward nonsense from start to finish. There was a very steep hill, we knew the Japs were on top, we knew they'd be in a reverse slope position and we were going to assault straight up the front – not a hope in hell! And there wasn't! *Lieutenant Sam Hornor, Signal Officer, HQ Coy, 2nd Norfolks*

The battalion was also vulnerable on the right flank.

Robert wasn't very happy about his right flank because it was uphill and the Japanese were on it. Very badly exposed. So we put mortars and machine guns on to it from the 2nd Manchesters. *Captain John Howard, Intelligence Officer, HQ, 4th Brigade*

Scott gave out his orders to his own 'O' Group – C Company would lead the attack immediately followed by A Company with B Company held in reserve. D Company would bring up the rear carrying reserve ammunition and entrenching tools for the consolidation of any positions captured. On 27 May the advanced companies moved into Aradura Nala drenched by pouring rain. Here they waited for confirmation that 6th Brigade was in position and ready to attack. Unfortunately they were having difficulty and the attack was of necessity postponed until 28 May. So at 03.15 on 28 May the Norfolks moved back into the Nala and began to feel their way through the jungle up Charles Hill. As they reached more open ground they came under considerable fire which pinned them down and the attack was halted. Soon new orders arrived as the Norfolks were ordered to disengage and move to the left to come in on the immediate right of the Royal Scots to attack Charles Hill from a different alignment. Walter Gilding, who had also been with B Echelon during the earlier phases of the fighting, was acting as Company Sergeant Major with B Company. They were to lead the attack, followed in by A Company. The attack started with an artillery bombardment at 16.10.

The company were lined up on the base of the hill, it was all jungle covered, not tracks leading up to it and it must have been about one in four. You couldn't walk up it, it had to be scrambled up, rather than walk, that kind of hill. The Royal Scots had a company on our left flank that was going to assist us. They fired solid shot from the 25 pounders so there was no danger to us the troops who were making the attack and hopefully this would break up the Japanese bunkers up on the crest of the hill. Everything was so quiet and peaceful. The idea was to put two platoons forward, side by side, to go up and the Royal Scots on our left flank were doing the same thing. You couldn't put a whole battalion in to a situation like that. Behind the reserve platoon were the company headquarters, me and my party. With us was Colonel Scott, helping organize the advance up the hill. We were all within touching distance – it was like that, there was no space to spread out as such. The artillery fired for a certain period of time and this allowed us to start scrambling up the hill. Bypassing a clump of bamboo, going round left or right of a tree, you couldn't just go straight up. We could hear the thudding of the shot into the top of the hill features. We got almost half way up, when the artillery stopped and then the fun began. Small arms fire, machine-gun fire and grenades – we got the lot. It was a matter of the troops going in to hopefully finish off the attack. *Company Sergeant Major Walter Gilding, B Coy, 2nd Norfolks*

B Company were assigned to the left flank of the attack

We went up the hill, it was very steep and there had been quite a lot of wet about the place. It was very difficult climbing and I didn't really see how anybody wearing army boots was going to get up there. In any case we all knew that the top was completely covered by Japanese fire from the hills behind. They were experts at that, all their bunker positions were covered by fire from other bunkers. We started scrambling up the side and then some Japanese grenades started coming down. So we threw our own grenades up to the top. I threw quite a lot and owing to the fact that the ground was so steep, there was a great danger of our grenades rolling back on us. So my inclination was to try and land my grenades on the very top, but if in doubt to go a little bit further so they wouldn't roll back. On my right our Company Commander, Richard Greene was going up on a slightly higher part and he got slightly shot. He did very well because that part was very heavily covered by fire. On the left where we were there was not quite so much. *Second Lieutenant Maurice Franses, B Coy, 2nd Norfolks*

The men clawed their way up the slippery slope.

> The leading lads had got within 20 feet of the top of the crest of the hill. It was absolutely hell, it was murder. Robert Scott had come up and he was with the leading troops throwing grenades like the clappers. Throwing them up and over, shouting, "Get on, get on, get at 'em!" By this time I was maybe ten yards at the most away from him. I had the Sten gun and I was firing, scrambling up, grabbing hold of a tree, firing the Sten gun, going a little further, encouraging the lads, saying, "Come along, get on, advance!" All this business, shouting, swearing... I wouldn't say I was frightened, I felt angry more than anything, just angry, wanting to really get in and finish it off. There was nothing to see at all, you couldn't see the bunker's slits or anything they were so well concealed. You can imagine scrambling up a hill, trying to find a bit of cover. I heard the stretcher bearers being called as people were getting hit. *Company Sergeant Major Walter Gilding, B Coy, 2nd Norfolks*

Franses was also using the Sten which he considered useful for such close-quarter jungle work.

> I had a Sten gun, I quite liked it, it was relatively lightweight, so it was mobile, one could if necessary fire with one hand by pushing the butt, such as there was into one's waist, you could turn round quickly and fire. There were reports of people suffering from the fact that the safety catches were not as reliable as they might be, but I think that was a better fault than the other way! *Second Lieutenant Maurice Franses, B Coy, 2nd Norfolks*

As the attack stalled just below the crest their Colonel once more moved into the thick of the action.

> Robert Scott got up there and he started throwing his grenades. He'd always been a very keen cricketer and when he was throwing these grenades he reminded me of a medium bowler lobbing them up there. He was being seen, that was important, it was a big help to us all, certainly it was a big help to me. I thought, "Well this is jolly good!" We had a report from one of the regiments over the other side of the valley, watching all this going on and they all saw Robert Scott doing his thing and they couldn't believe what they were seeing, him standing upright and chucking the grenades, ducking and so forth. *Second Lieutenant Maurice Franses, B Coy, 2nd Norfolks*

From their positions on the top of the hill in any grenade throwing exchange the Japanese had a natural advantage.

You could hear the grenades going off, Bren guns firing, Japanese light machine guns firing... It seemed as though the Japs were just sat on the top of the ridge just rolling blooming hand grenades down. *Bugler Bert May, HQ Coy, 2nd Norfolks*

Some of the men sought to return the grenades to sender but it was a 'game' fraught with risk.

You'd hear them knock their grenades on their tin hats to start the firing pin. You'd say, "Grenades!" They'd come over, you'd pick it up, throw it back! Because they had 10 second fuses on theirs' so therefore we had time to pick them up. If you saw it come when it came – and if it was the same grenade as the one you heard. *Private William Cron, Carrier Platoon, HQ Coy, 2nd Norfolks*

In the middle of this maelstrom of bullets and grenades Scott's phenomenal luck ran out at last.

After a few minutes of this, a Japanese grenade came down towards Robert Scott and I think he decided to kick it away. He misjudged slightly, it went off and brought him down. *Second Lieutenant Maurice Franses, B Coy, 2nd Norfolks*

The stretcher bearers now had a real problem on their hands.

I saw him go down and the stretcher bearers come to try pick him up. They cut his trousers open to put a field dressing on his wounds. This uncovered his bottom and through all the noise that was going on Robert shouted out, "COVER MY BLOODY ARSE UP!" *Company Sergeant Major Walter Gilding, B Coy, 2nd Norfolks*

Shouting and bawling Scott was carried down the hill.

I saw him on a stretcher coming down. He was shouting and cursing because the lads wouldn't let him off – he wanted to get off the stretcher! But he couldn't, a hand grenade had landed at his feet, he was just peppered all over with shrapnel. It took about eight blokes to carry him, anyone grabbed a handle and helped. You can imagine the weight of him, because he was a big bloke, and the ground itself wasn't given to carrying stretchers up and down believe me! We helped, I got the side of the stretcher and carried it, helped to keep him on. But he was doing his nut he was, shouting blue murder! We got him down and took him to the first aid post. *Bugler Bert May, HQ Coy, 2nd Norfolks*

Bert May

Behind him Private Cron and others were covering the stretcher bearer party as best they could.

I had a go at the Japs with my Bren gun, kept their heads down while the stretcher bearers got him out. If somebody hadn't fired on the bunkers they'd have popped him and the stretcher bearers off. So I had two magazines of 30 rounds each and I gave them the full 60 up the hill. I got one through the arm – it didn't do much harm – it didn't stop me from carrying on firing. By that time they'd got the old man on to the stretcher and were getting him down into cover. *Private William Cron, Carrier Platoon, HQ Coy, 2nd Norfolks*

Young Second Lieutenant Franses, who was in his first fully fledged battle, was inspired by the example his Colonel had set.

The reaction on me was really quite remarkable. That is a sign of the man he was. Because as soon as he was down, I felt I had to take over, he had created such an impression. I shouted, "Come on, chaps, the COs down but we've still got a job to do!" or something like that. In a way that was my high moment of the war, I think, I really felt that there was a man who had shown a wonderful example and one just had to follow it, there was no choice at all. *Second Lieutenant Maurice Franses, B Coy, 2nd Norfolks*

All along the ridge such men sought by one last effort to get to the top of the ridge – sought to justify the sacrifice of their comrades.

At the same time a Bren gunner on my flank got hit and the Bren gun slithered down alongside me. I picked it up and carried on. I had one arm round a tree and one arm pressing the Bren gun into a big clump of earth alongside me firing it from there. What good it was doing I don't know but it was relieving me anyway! After firing a few bursts, the situation was hopeless, Robert had been taken down to the bottom of the hill by the stretcher bearers and Murray-Brown took over. He came up on the scene and ordered everybody to withdraw off the hill. No way would we have got to the top. It was hopeless. I think I was one of the last to come off because I had the Bren gun and I thought was giving covering fire. Murray-Brown called out to me, "Sergeant Major, get down! Get down!" *Company Sergeant Major Walter Gilding, B Coy, 2nd Norfolks*

Major William Murray-Brown, one of the survivors of the campaign in France who had tasted defeat, no matter how glorious, recognized that it was futile. He reluctantly conceded failure and ordered the suspension of the attack. Cron was another of the rear guard.

I thought, "Right, its time for me to get out because there's only me here now – everybody else has gone!" I turned and made a

William Murray-Bro

214

dash because I'd no more ammunition. I scarpered more or less head over heals down the hill. As I dashed off one of the Jap bullets hit my pack and set off a smoke grenade. So I had to jettison my pack for fear of it causing me damage. I got down behind the bushes where they were. Then they saw the blood trickling out of my arm and they said, "Right" They pinned a label on my tunic and said, "Get in the ambulance – off you go!" *Private William Cron, Carrier Platoon, HQ Coy, 2nd Norfolks*

The defeated Norfolks were shattered as they fell back across the Aradura Nala to GPT Ridge.

I tried to sleep, but couldn't and I was shaking, that was the reaction to the battle. *Company Sergeant Major Walter Gilding, B Coy, 2nd Norfolks*

Most were grateful just to be alive. They had lived under awful conditions in extreme danger ever since they began the 'trek' round to GPT Ridge a whole month earlier on 25 April.

There were times when you got overcome by despair and some chaps thought that if they got a bullet through the bloody head that was a happy release. It does get you down. You have to experience it, you can't describe anything like that, you have to experience it. It's like trying to describe a pain. However sympathetic you are, you can't envisage it, can't visualise what it's like. You can see it on films, read it in books, but you have to actually experience the pain, suffering and all those other things that a soldier has to endure in wartime. You're so sick and fed up of the whole bloody thing. You want to get it over, you want to come home. As far as you're concerned you're all suffering, and nobody, but nobody, suffers more than you. You're all equal. There are exceptionally brave men, I don't know how you define bravery. I think everybody's brave who was out there. You've got to be bloody brave to suffer it because under normal circumstances I think a bloke would say, "Bugger this!" and turn tail and scuttle off. To lie there and let some bloody sod lob bloody shells at you to try and kill you! You think to yourself, "I must be bloody nuts doing this!" But you do it because your mates are doing it. *Private Dick Fiddament, 2nd Norfolks*

It was obvious that the Norfolks could do no more and the exhausted survivors were sent by transport along the cleared Kohima road to the base at Dimapur for a week of well earned rest.

When it was all over you just felt, "Thank God!"

Bugler Bert May, HQ Coy, 2nd Norfolks

Overall at Kohima 11 officers and 79 other ranks had been killed with a further 13 officers and over 150 ranks wounded. In the chaos and

Japanese troops on Aradura Spur resisted the heroic efforts of the Norfolks.

mayhem of the Kohima fighting many had not fully appreciated just
how many friends they had lost.

> You don't think. It's:
>
>> "Here's to the dead already
>>
>> Here's to the last man to die"
>
> You don't feel it. *Captain Dickie Davies, 2nd Norfolks*

The impact of the death of his friend David Glasse and the misery
suffered by his wife Louise only really hit John Howard several months
later when he returned to visit his grave.

> At the time it was a dull blow. So many died that the loss of
> individuals was softened. In the following November, I visited the
> Divisional Cemetery where the long rows of familiar names on the
> crosses filled me with a loneliness that I had not felt when they
> died.[19] *Captain John Howard, Intelligence Officer HQ, 4th Brigade*

The battalion erected a memorial to their dead between GPT Ridge and

Aradura Spur. Another to the whole of the 2nd Division was unveiled at Kohima. The inscription has since come to epitomize the entire British struggle and the poignant loneliness of their losses deep in the inhospitable jungle. It is known as the Kohima Prayer.

> **When you go home**
> **Tell them of us and say,**
> **For your tomorrow**
> **We gave our today**.

Although they had failed to storm Aradura Ridge the Norfolks had without doubt played a glorious part in the long battle of Kohima. The wild Assam country could 'swallow' a whole division almost without trace in its jungles, mountains and precipitous ravines. Yet those same dramatic geographical features meant that a well sited Japanese platoon concealed in cross firing bunkers could hold up a whole brigade. In these circumstances the importance of a platoon, company or battalion attack could be crucial to the whole of a divisional push. Hence the dramatic success on 4 May when the Norfolks cleared GPT Ridge by coup de main. It did not in fact, as was hoped, solve the problems of the other units fighting to clear the Kohima Ridge, but it did mark a huge step forward. The Norfolks triumphed that day, but that very success sowed the pyrrhic seeds of defeat. The steady drip of casualties gradually eroded the bedrock of the unit and so at each step left it ever more likely to fall at the next hurdle. So the Norfolks' capture of GPT Ridge led inexorably to their increasing problems in front of the somewhat ironically named 'Norfolk Bunker' and to their subsequent heroic failure on the precipitous slopes of Aradura Spur – a ridge too far. But the Norfolks had together pushed themselves to the limits of human endurance and in doing so had played a pivotal role in the British victory of Kohima. This in conjunction with the heroic efforts of so many other British and Indian units in the besieged Imphal box cemented the British Empire's grip on India.

Yet the Battle of Kohima was not the end for the Norfolks. It was just another staging post in the war. There was no easy 'end' to the fighting. Within little more than a week the newly reinforced Norfolks were fighting and dying on yet another Assam ridge – Viswema. One battle led inexorably to another. No infantryman could ever feel safe in the front line until the war was over and the last bullet fired. The hero of one attack was often the tragically maimed or dying casualty at the next. And so began the long, long weary blood soaked road to Mandalay. But let the final word lie with an ordinary soldier.

I wasn't no hero, no gung ho man, like everyone else I did what

I had to and that was it. We didn't want any special pats on the back. Without the infantry soldier there would be no end to war. Wars are started and fought – they have to be finished. The Royal Air Force were magnificent, the bombing raids they did, the acts of bravery the fighter pilots performed. Wars fought at sea, submariners, all branches of the services had men who performed acts of bravery above and beyond the call of duty. But the point I try to make is that if he gets through that particular action he returns to his base and has a certain form of comfort, he's out of the picture for a time, however brief. But the infantry soldier once he's engaged with the enemy it can go on for weeks, months – in this case in Burma for 12-14 months. You have brief periods of rest but you are then embroiled in this horrific, horrendous confrontation with somebody who will use every means at his disposal to hasten your demise. In the end it all comes down to the infantry soldier that has to go in and finally capture, and consolidate that position. I don't mean in any sense to make out that the infantry soldier is the be-all and end-all. Of course you had the Royal Army Service Corps doing a magnificent job bringing up rations; the Royal Engineers who built bridges, blew up bridges, did a magnificent job; the Royal Corps of Signals, without which we couldn't exist. You had to be supplied, fed and nurtured by these different types of regiments. None-the-less the actual eye to eye contact finally has to be completed by the infantry soldier. *Private Dick Fiddament, 2nd Norfolks.*

1 . D E Jones, Royal Norfolk Regiment Museum, File 22
2 . D E Jones, Royal Norfolk Regiment Museum, File 22
3 . *Britannia Magazine*, Murray Brown had obviously expanded upon the Battalion War Diary kept by Captain C W H Long held at Royal Norfolk Regiment Museum, File 22
4 . Lance Sergeant Aldin, Royal Norfolk Regiment Museum, File 22
5 . Albert Pooley quoted in Cyril Jolly, *The Vengeance of Private Pooley*, (Heinemann, London, 1956), pp IX.

6 . IWM DOCS, John Howard, *Kohima to Mandalay*

7 . IWM DOCS, John Howard, *Kohima to Mandalay*

8 . IWM DOCS, John Howard, *Kohima to Mandalay*

9 . IWM DOCS, John Howard, *Kohima to Mandalay*

10 . IWM DOCS, John Howard, *Kohima to Mandalay*

11 . Sam Hornor, quoted in Arthur Swinson, *Kohima*, (Cassell, London, 1966), pp121-122.

12 . IWM DOCS, John Howard, *Kohima to Mandalay*

13 . IWM DOCS, John Howard, *Kohima to Mandalay*

14 . IWM DOCS, John Howard, *Kohima to Mandalay*

15 . IWM DOCS, John Howard, *Kohima to Mandalay*

16 . IWM DOCS, John Howard, *Kohima to Mandalay*

17 . IWM DOCS, John Howard, *Kohima to Mandalay*

18 . IWM DOCS, John Howard, *Kohima to Mandalay*

19 . IWM DOCS, John Howard, *Kohima to Mandalay*

Medals presented to those who had been seen to do well. Here Sergeant Davies is decorated by the Viceroy of India Field Marshal Lord Wavell. He had been shot in the leg during the attack on 4th May but stayed in action until the situation was resolved. It was not his first award for bravery he had received the MM for his work in the first patrol of the war with Peter Barclay back in 1940. IWM IND 3656

Dedication of the 2nd Norfolk's Memorial at Kohima.

When you go home, tell them of us...

The long and winding trail to Mandalay and then Rangoon. Many more Norfolks were to die before the Japanese were finally defeated in Burma.

Taylor Library

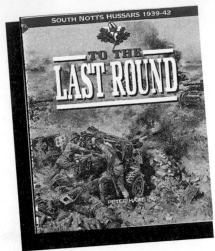

First in the popular series of
battalion histories of the
Second World War – based upon
oral records held in the Imperial
War Museum Sound Archive

TO THE

LAST ROUND

SOUTH NOTTS HUSSARS 1939-42

by Peter Hart

This is the exciting story of an artillery unit, raised in Nottinghamshire, which fought panzers of Rommel's Afrika Korps over the open sights of their 25 pounders at the Battle of Knightsbridge. Whilst other units withdrew they were ordered to 'fight to the last round', which order they dutifully complied with. The immense power of the narrative is provided by the very words of the survivors. *To The Last Round* is a detailed portrayal of life in an artillery regiment in the Second World War.

ISBN: 0-85052-514-4   £17.95

Available from booksellers and direct from the publisher:

Pen & Sword Books Limited
47 Church Street
Barnsley
South Yorkshire S70 2AS
Telephone 01226 734555
Fax: 01226 734438
Email: charles@pen-and-sword.demon.co.uk
World Wide Web Site: http://www.yorkshire-web.co.uk/ps/